Abingdon's

Where the Bible Comes to Life

Preschool 7

New Life

Also available from Abingdon Press:

Abingdon's BibleZone®
Preschool 7
FUNspirational® Kit

Abingdon's BibleZone®
Younger Elementary 7
Teacher's Guide
Abingdon's BibleZone®
Younger Elementary 7
FUNspirational® Kit

Abingdon's BibleZone®
Older Elementary 7
Teacher's Guide
Abingdon's BibleZone®
Older Elementary 7
FUNspirational® Kit

Writer/Editor: Daphna Flegal
Production Editor: Betsi Hoey Smith
Production and Design Manager:
R. E. Osborne
Designer: Paige Easter
Cover Photo: Sid Dorris
Illustrator: Robert S. Jones

Abingdon's

Bible Zone

Preschool

Where the Bible Comes to Life

NEW LIFE

Abingdon Press
Nashville

Abingdon's
BibleZone®
Where the Bible Comes to Life
Preschool 7

Copyright © 1999 Abingdon Press

All rights reserved.

No part of this work, EXCEPT PATTERNS AND PAGES COVERED BY THE FOLLOWING NOTICE, may be reproduced or transmitted in any form or by any means, electronic or mechanical, including photocopying and recording, or by any information storage or retrieval system, except as may be expressly permitted by the 1976 Copyright Act or in writing from the publisher. Requests for permission should be addressed in writing to
Abingdon Press, 201 Eighth Avenue South, Nashville, TN 37203.

ISBN 0-687-093511

Unless otherwise noted, Scripture quotations are from the New Revised Standard Version of the Bible.
Copyright © 1989 by the Division of Christian Education
of the National Council of Churches of Christ in the USA.
Used by permission.

Scripture quotations identified as *Good News Bible*
are from the *Good News Bible: The Bible in Today's English Version*.
Old Testament: Copyright © American Bible Society 1976, 1992;
New Testament: Copyright © American Bible Society 1966, 1971, 1976, 1992
Used by permission.

ANY PATTERN may be reproduced for use in the local church or church school provided it is marked as **Reproducible** and the following copyright notice is included:
Permission granted to copy for local church use. © 1999 Abingdon Press.

A Cassette accompanies this resource and can be found in the FUNspirational® Kit (0-687-094712). On the Cassette are all masters ℗ Brentwood Music, Inc. and Benson Records, Inc. both divisions of the Provident Music Group, One Maryland Farms, Brentwood, TN 37207. All rights reserved. Used by permission. Unauthorized duplication prohibited.

99 00 01 02 03 04 05 06 07 08–10 9 8 7 6 5 4 3 2 1
MANUFACTURED IN THE UNITED STATES OF AMERICA

Table of Contents
New Life

Bible Units in the Zone 6
About BibleZone® 7
Welcome to the BibleZone® 8
Preschoolers 9
Shout Hosanna! 10
Wash My Feet 22
Remember Me 34
Jesus Lives! 46
Do You Believe? 58
In the Beginning 70
Sun, Moon, Stars 82
Fish and Birds 94
Animals 106
In God's Image 118
Adam and Eve 130
The Naming 142
For Everything a Season 154
BirthdayZone 166
Birthday Banner 167
ClayZone 168
The Bible Zone 169
SongZone 170
SnackZone 171
Nametags 172
All About You 173
BZ Bee Puppet 174
Comments from Users 175

Bible Units in the Zone

Use these suggestions if you choose to organize the lessons in short-term units.

New Life in Jesus

Bible Story	Bible Verse
Shout Hosanna!	Hosanna! John 12:13
Wash My Feet	Love one another. John 13:34
Remember Me	Do this in memory of me. Luke 22:19, *Good News Bible*
Jesus Lives!	See, everything has become new! 2 Corinthians 5:17
Do You Believe?	Stop your doubting, and believe! John 20:27, *Good News Bible*

New Life in God's World

Bible Story	Bible Verse
In the Beginning	And God saw that it was good. Genesis 1:25
Sun, Moon, Stars	And God saw that it was good. Genesis 1:25
Fish and Birds	And God saw that it was good. Genesis 1:25
Animals	And God saw that it was good. Genesis 1:25
In God's Image	And God saw that it was good. Genesis 1:25
Adam and Eve	God made us, and we belong to God. Psalm 100:3, *Good News Bible*, adapted
The Naming	O Lord, our Lord, your greatness is seen in all the world. Psalm 8:1, *Good News Bible*
For Everything a Season	For everything there is a season. Ecclesiastes 3:1

About BibleZone

ZoneZillies:

ZoneZillies® are game and storytelling props found in the BibleZone® FUNspirational® Kit. Some ZoneZillies® are consumable and will need to be replaced. These are added for the teacher's convenience.

- rock ball
- fan
- zoo finger puppets
- binoculars
- plastic ducks
- inflatable celestial ball
- inflatable dolphin ring toss
- lamb puppet
- green crepe paper roll
- modeling clay
- bird stickers
- fish stickers
- luminous chalk
- flashlight (requires one AA battery not included)
- Cassette with music by Brentwood Kids Music

Not recommended for children under 3.

Supplies:

- Bible
- cassette player
- one AA battery
- construction paper
- glue
- safety scissors
- clear plastic tape
- masking tape
- stapler, staples
- crayons or markers
- colored chalk
- sponges
- water
- paint drop cloth, old shower curtains, or large towels
- Bibletimes headdress
- basin of warm, sudsy water; washcloth; towel
- newspapers
- small and large paper plates
- bag
- paper towels
- napkins
- tempera paint
- shallow trays
- sandal
- crayons with papers removed
- jar of water
- uncut hoagie roll
- glass of grape juice or red punch
- Communion plate or cup
- smocks
- milk or juice jug lids, empty thread spools, film canisters or cardboard rolls
- grapes
- ingredients for play dough (see page 168)
- blanket
- drinking straws
- marbles
- cup or plastic bowl
- cotton swabs
- green icing, sugar cones, red cinnamon candies

Welcome to the BibleZone

Where the Bible Comes to Life

Have fun learning about new life. Each lesson in this teacher guide is filled with games and activities that will make learning FUNspirational® for you and your children. With just a few added supplies, everything you need to teach is included in the Abingdon's BibleZone® FUNspirational® Kit. You may want to add BZ Bee, a colorful and plush hand puppet that the children will love (see page 174). BZ Bee helps teach the Bible verse each week in the *ZoneIn® with BZ Bee* section.

Each lesson has a ZoneIn® box:

 We praise God for Jesus and for new life.

that is repeated over and over again throughout the lesson. The ZoneIn® states the Bible message in words your children will understand.

Use the following tips to help make your trip into the BibleZone® a FUNspirational® success!
- Read through each lesson. Read the Bible passages.
- Memorize the Bible verse and the ZoneIn® statement.
- Choose activities that fit your unique group of children and your time limitations.
- Practice telling the BibleZone® story.
- Gather the ZoneZillies® you will use for the lesson.
- Gather supplies you will use for the lesson.
- Learn the music for the lesson from the BibleZone® FUNspirational® Cassette. Side 1 contains songs that celebrate new life in Jesus. Side 2 contains songs that thank God for Creation.
- Arrange your room space to fit the lesson. Move tables and chairs so there is plenty of room for the children to move and sit on the floor.
- Copy the Reproducible pages for the lesson.
- Copy the HomeZone® page for Parents.
- Copy the nametags (page 172), All About You page (page 173), and birthday page (page 167) to use as needed with your class.

Preschoolers

Each child in your class is a one-of-a-kind child of God. Each child has his or her own name, background, family situation, and set of experiences. It is important to remember and celebrate the uniqueness of each child. Yet all of these one-of-a-kind children of God have some common needs.

- All children need love.
- All children need a sense of self-worth.
- All children need to feel a sense of accomplishment.
- All children need to have a safe place to be and to express their feelings.
- All children need to be surrounded by adults who love them.
- All children need to experience the love of God.

Preschoolers (children ages 3-5 years old) also have some common characteristics.

Their Bodies
- They do not sit still for very long.
- They have lots of energy.
- They enjoy moving (running, galloping, dancing, jumping, hopping).
- They are developing fine motor skills (learning to cut with scissors, learning to handle a ball, learning to tie their shoes).
- They enjoy using their senses (taste, touch, smell, hearing, seeing).

Their Minds
- They are learning more and more words.
- They enjoy music.
- They are learning to express their feelings.
- They like to laugh and be silly.
- They enjoy nonsense words.
- They are learning to identify colors, sizes, and shapes.
- They have an unclear understanding of time.
- They have a wonderful imagination.

Their Relationships
- They are beginning to interact with others as they play together.
- They are beginning to understand that other people have feelings.
- They are learning to wait for their turn.
- They can have a hard time leaving parents, especially mother.
- They want to help.
- They love to feel important.

Their Hearts
- They need to handle the Bible and see others handle it.
- They need caring adults who model Christian attitudes and behaviors.
- They need to sing, move to, and say Bible verses.
- They need to hear clear, simple stories from the Bible.
- They can express simple prayers.
- They can experience wonder and awe at God's world.
- They can share food and money and make things for others.
- They can experience belonging at church.

1 Bible

Shout Hosanna!

Enter the Zone

Bible Verse
Hosanna!
        John 12:13

Bible Story
John 12:12-15

At the time of Jesus' triumphal entry into Jerusalem, the city and the entire Palestine area were under Roman control. Even though the Jewish people resented the oppressive Roman government, they were given a certain amount of freedom. This included religious freedom. Because of this the Jewish leaders were sensitive to any disturbance that might cause them to revoke this order. Passover was a very precarious time. The city was filled with thousands of tourists from all over the world who had come to celebrate. Into the midst of this turbulent time, a man on a donkey came to town.

It was no accident that Jesus entered Jerusalem riding a donkey. The people were hoping for a king to rescue them from Roman oppression. If Jesus had ridden a horse, he would have been sending a message of military greatness. The donkey symbolized peace. Jesus was not denying that he was the chosen king, but he was showing that his kingdom was a peaceful one. The people draped the donkey and covered the road with cloaks, just as they would welcome a new king.

The Gospel of John tells us that when the people saw Jesus, they went out to meet him, waving palm branches and shouting,

"Hosanna!
Blessed is the one who comes in
   the name of the Lord—
the King of Israel!" (John 12:13)

"Hosanna," which means "save us," was a prayer asking for God's help. "Hosanna" was also a cry of triumph. The word probably had both meanings as the people watched Jesus ride into Jerusalem.

Young children love celebrations and parades. Because young children are concrete thinkers, they may not be able to understand the symbolism of this Bible story. They can, however, enjoy the celebration of their friend, Jesus.

We praise God for Jesus and for new life.

Scope the Zone

ZONE	TIME	SUPPLIES	ZILLIES®
Zoom Into the Zone			
Ear He Comes	10 minutes	Reproducible 1A, scissors, tape or glue, crayons	none
Sing 'n Shout	5 minutes	Reproducible 1A	none
BibleZone®			
Praise Parade	5 minutes	none	none
Shout "Hosanna!"	10 minutes	Reproducible 1A	none
Bible Verse Buzz	5 minutes	Bible, BZ Bee	none
Sing!	5 minutes	cassette player	Cassette, green crepe paper
LifeZone			
Green on Green	10 minutes	green construction paper, glue	green crepe paper
Hop Hop Hosanna	10 minutes	Reproducible 1B, scissors, masking tape, cassette player	Cassette
Shout "Hosanna!"	5 minutes	Reproducible 1B, scissors	none
Puppet Prayers	5 minutes	none	lamb puppet

⊙ Zillies® are found in the **BibleZone® FUNspirational® Kit.**

Zoom Into the Zone

Choose one or more activities to catch your children's interest.

Supplies:
Reproducible 1A, scissors, tape or glue, crayons

Zillies®:
none

Ear He Comes

Photocopy and cut apart the donkey ears and headband **(Reproducible 1A)** for each child before class begins. Tape or glue the ends of each headband together to make one long strip.

Give each child a pair of donkey ears and a headband strip. Let the children decorate the ears and strips with crayons. Show each child how to tape or glue the donkey ears onto the headband strip so that the ears hang down on each side of the child's head. Measure the strip around each child's head. Tape the ends of the strip together. Encourage the children to wear their donkey ears.

Say: Today our Bible story is about the time when Jesus rode a donkey into the city. The people were happy to see Jesus. They waved palm branches and shouted praise to God.

 **We praise God for Jesus and for new life.**

Supplies:
Reproducible 1A

Zillies®:
none

Sing 'n Shout

Have the children wear their donkey ears **(Reproducible 1A)** and stand in a circle.

Say: When Jesus rode a donkey into the city, the people were happy to see Jesus. They waved palm branches and shouted, "Hosanna!"

Sing the song printed below to the tune of "She'll Be Coming 'Round the Mountain." Lead the children in doing the motions as you sing. Shout the word *Hosanna*!

(Pretend to ride a donkey.)
He'll be riding on a donkey
 when he comes,
He'll be riding on a donkey
 when he comes.
He'll be riding on a donkey,
He'll be riding on a donkey,
He'll be riding on a donkey
 when he comes.

(Wave arms in the air.)
O we'll all shout **"Hosanna!"**
 when he comes,
O we'll all shout **"Hosanna!"**
 when he comes.
O we'll all shout **"Hosanna!"**,
We'll all shout **"Hosanna!"**,
O we'll all shout **"Hosanna!"**
 when he comes.

BibleZone®

Choose one or more activities to immerse your children in the Bible story.

Praise Parade

 se the following parade to lead your children around the room. Repeat the verses as necessary to lead the children to your story area.

Supplies:
none

Zillies®:
none

Here comes the praise parade.
(March around the room.)
Here comes the praise parade.
Follow me and march, march, march.
Here comes the praise parade.

Praise God, praise God,
(Stop marching; hold arms above head and shake hands.)
Let's praise God for Jesus.
(Clap hands.)
Praise God, praise God,
(Hold arms above head and shake hands.)
Let's praise God today.
(Clap hands.)
Hurray!
(Hold arms up above head and jump.)

Here comes the praise parade.
(Stomp around the room.)
Here comes the praise parade.
Follow me and stomp, stomp, stomp.
Here comes the praise parade.

Praise God, praise God,
(Stop stomping; hold arms above head and shake hands.)
Let's praise God for Jesus.
(Clap hands.)
Praise God, praise God,
(Hold arms above head and shake hands.)
Let's praise God today.
(Clap hands.)
Hurray!
(Hold arms up above head and jump.)

Bible Zone Story

Shout Hosanna!

by Sharilyn S. Adair

 ncourage the children to wear their donkey ears (**Reproducible 1A**) and to stand in a circle in your story area.

Say: One day Jesus and his followers were going to Jerusalem to visit the Temple, which is like a big church building. They were going to celebrate the Passover, one of their special holidays. Something exciting happened on the way. When they were near Jerusalem, Jesus asked two of his followers to get him a donkey to ride into the city, and they did. The donkey was a very young donkey. When Jesus rode on the donkey, the people cheered and waved palm branches all along the way. Today's story is a poem about that day. Listen and do as I do.

Little Donkey,
(Touch donkey ears or place one fist on each side of your head, with your index fingers pointing up like donkey ears.)
Clippity clop!
(Slap your thighs in a clip-clop rhythm.)
Who is that you have on top?
(Raise hands and shrug shoulders.)

Little Donkey,
(Touch donkey ears.)
Walk with care.
(Walk in place.)
Jesus is your rider there.
(Pretend to hold reins and ride donkey.)

Little Donkey,
(Touch donkey ears.)
Don't be late.
(Walk in place more rapidly.)
Take him to the city gate.
(Pretend to hold reins and ride donkey.)

Little Donkey,
(Touch donkey ears.)
See the crowd
(Place one hand over your eyes and move head from side to side as though searching.)
Wave their palms and shout out loud.
(Wave one arm over head.)

Little Donkey,
(Touch donkey ears.)
Hear them say,
(Cup one hand behind one ear.)
"Hosanna to the Lord!" today.
(Wave one arm over head.)

Little Donkey,
(Touch donkey ears.)
Hear them say,
(Cup one hand behind one ear.)
"Hosanna to the Lord!" today.
(Wave one arm over head.)

In With BZ Bee

Bible Verse Buzz

Choose a child to hold the Bible open to John 12:13.

Say: Today our Bible story is about the time when Jesus rode a donkey into the city. The people were happy to see Jesus. They waved palm branches and shouted, "Hosanna!"

Say the Bible verse, "Hosanna!" (John 12:13), for the children. Have the children say the Bible verse after you.

Turn your back to the children or hide your hands underneath a table or behind the **BibleZone® FUNspirational® Kit** lid as you place the **BZ Bee puppet** (see page 174) on your hand. Turn around or bring the puppet out where the children can see it.

Pretend to make the puppet talk. Change your voice for the puppet:

Bzzz. Bzzz. Bzzz. Hi, everybody! I'm BZ Bee. *Bzzz. Bzzz. Bzzz.* I like to taste fingers. Do you have fingers? Yum, yum, yum. Let me taste.

Go to each child. Encourage, but do not force, each child to hold up his or her fingers. Have BZ pretend to taste each child's fingers. Have BZ say things like:

Mmmm. Mmmm. You taste like honey.
Bzzz. Bzzz. You taste like strawberries.
Yumm. Yumm. You taste like blueberries.

After BZ has tasted each child's fingers, say:

Bzzz. Bzzz. Bzzz. I like to taste your fingers. They're yummy. *(Rub BZ's stomach.)*

Bzzz. Bzzz. Bzzz. I like something else even more than fingers.

I like the Bible. *Bzzz. Bzzz. Bzzz.* You heard a Bible story today. Who rode the donkey into the city? *(Jesus)* What did the people shout when they saw Jesus? *(Hosanna!)*

Bzzz. Bzzz. Bzzz. The people were happy to see Jesus. They shouted, "Hosanna!" to praise God for Jesus.

 **We praise God for Jesus and for new life.**

Bzzz. Bzzz. Bzzz. Let's say the Bible verse together.

"Hosanna!" (John 12:13).

Have the children repeat the Bible verse with BZ Bee.

Have BZ Bee say good-bye to the children. Put the puppet away.

Bible

Choose one or more activities to immerse your children in the Bible story.

Supplies:
cassette player

Zillies®:
Cassette, green crepe paper

Sing!

Have the children move to an open area of the room. Tear off strips of **green crepe paper** to make streamers. Give each child one or two streamers.

Say: When Jesus rode a donkey into the city, the people were happy to see Jesus. They waved palm branches and shouted, "Hosanna!" Let's pretend our green streamers are green palm branches. Let's wave our streamers to a song of praise. Let's praise God for Jesus and for new life.

Play the song "Praise, Praise, Praise" on the **Cassette**.

Praise, Praise, Praise

I love to praise, praise, praise in so many, many ways.
Praise, praise, praise Him day and night.
I love to praise, praise, praise in so many, many ways.
Praise Him with my heart and soul and might.

I love to sing a song way up high,
Lift my hands to the sky-yi!
Whisper softly, shout out loud!
Whistle a melody, *(whistle)*
Hum a tune happily! *(Hm-hm-hm-hm-hmm)*

I love to praise, praise, praise in so many, many ways.
Praise, praise, praise Him day and night.
I love to praise, praise, praise in so many, many ways.
Praise Him with my heart and soul and might.

Praise him with my heart and soul and might!

Writer: Janet McMahan-Wilson
© 1995 New Spring Publishing/ASCAP
All Rights Reserved
Used by permission of Brentwood-Benson Music Publishing, Inc.

From Brentwood Music, Inc. recording *God's Way A Song A Day, vol. 2.*

Life Zone

Choose one or more activities to bring the Bible to life.

Green on Green

Give each child a piece of green construction paper and a **green crepe paper** strip.

Say: When Jesus rode a donkey into the city, the people were happy to see Jesus. They waved palm branches and shouted, "Hosanna!" Let's pretend our green streamers are green palm branches.

Show the children how to tear their crepe paper strips into small pieces. Let the children glue the pieces onto their construction paper any way that they wish.

Say: The people praised God for Jesus and for new life.

Supplies:
green construction paper, glue

Zillies®:
green crepe paper

We can praise God for Jesus and for new life.

Hop Hop Hosanna

Photocopy and cut apart the palm branch cards (**Reproducible 1B**). You will need as many cards as you have children. Place the palm branch cards on the floor in a circle. Secure the cards to the floor with masking tape. Show the children the palm branch cards. Help the children count how many palm branches are pictured on each card.

Say: When Jesus rode a donkey into the city, the people were happy to see Jesus. They waved palm branches and shouted, "Hosanna!"

Have the children walk around the circle of palm branch cards as you play music from the **Cassette**. Stop the music. Have each child stand on a palm branch card. Call each child by name one at a time. Help each child count how many palm branches are pictured on the card.

Say: *(Child's name)*, **hop up and down** *(number of palm branches pictured on the card)* **times.**

Play the game again as time and interest allow.

Supplies:
Reproducible 1B, scissors, masking tape, cassette player

Zillies®:
Cassette

PRESCHOOL 7

Choose one or more activities to bring the Bible to life.

Supplies:
Reproducible 1B, scissors

Zillies®:
none

Shout Hosanna

hotocopy and cut apart one set of the palm branch cards (**Reproducible 1B**). Have the children sit on the floor.

Say: When Jesus rode a donkey into the city, the people were happy to see Jesus. They waved palm branches and shouted, "Hosanna!" Let's look at the palm branches on these cards. When I hold up a card with one palm branch, shout "Hosanna!" one time. When I hold up a card with two palm branches, shout "Hosanna!" two times. When I hold up a card with three palm branches, how many times will you shout "Hosanna!"? *(three times)* **What if I hold up a card with four palm branches?** *(Shout "Hosanna!" four times.)*

Hold up each card. Have the children shout "Hosanna!" the number of times the palm branches are pictured on the card.

Supplies:
none

Zillies®:
lamb puppet

Puppet Prayers

ave the children sit down. Show the children the **lamb puppet**.

Say: This is my puppet, Lambkins. What kind of animal is Lambkins? *(lamb, sheep)* **Lambs help us remember the new life God plans for us in God's world. Lambs can also help us remember that Jesus taught us about new life. Lambkins wants to help us praise God for Jesus and new life.**

Hold up the lamb puppet and sing the following song to the tune of "Are You Sleeping?" Pretend that the puppet is singing one line, and have the children sing the repeating line after the puppet.

Here is Lambkins,
Here is Lambkins,
Come to say,
Come to say,
"Let's praise God for Jesus
"Let's praise God for Jesus
As we pray."
As we pray."

Pray: Thank you, God, for Jesus. Thank you, God, for new life. Amen.

Photocopy the **HomeZone®** newsletter to send home to parents.

Home Zone For Parents

Bible Verse
Hosanna!
John 12:13

Bible Story
John 12:12-15

Shout Hosanna

Today your child heard the Bible story of when Jesus rode a donkey into the city of Jerusalem. When the people saw Jesus, they welcomed Jesus as they would welcome a king. They waved palm branches and shouted, "Hosanna!"

"Hosanna," which means "save us," was a prayer asking for God's help. "Hosanna" was also a cry of triumph.

Young children love celebrations and parades. Enjoy the celebration of your friend, Jesus, with your child.

Sing 'n Shout

Sing the song printed below to the tune of "She'll Be Coming 'Round the Mountain." Let your child do the motions as you sing the song together. Shout the word, "Hosanna!"

(Pretend to ride a donkey.)
He'll be riding on a donkey when he comes,
He'll be riding on a donkey when he comes.
He'll be riding on a donkey, he'll be riding on a donkey,
He'll be riding on a donkey when he comes.

(Wave arms in the air.)
O we'll all shout **"Hosanna!"** when he comes,
O we'll all shout **"Hosanna!"** when he comes.
O we'll all shout **"Hosanna!"**, we'll all shout **"Hosanna!"**,
O we'll all shout **"Hosanna!"** when he comes.

We praise God for Jesus and for new life.

PRESCHOOL 7   Permission granted to photocopy for local church use. © 1999 Abingdon Press.

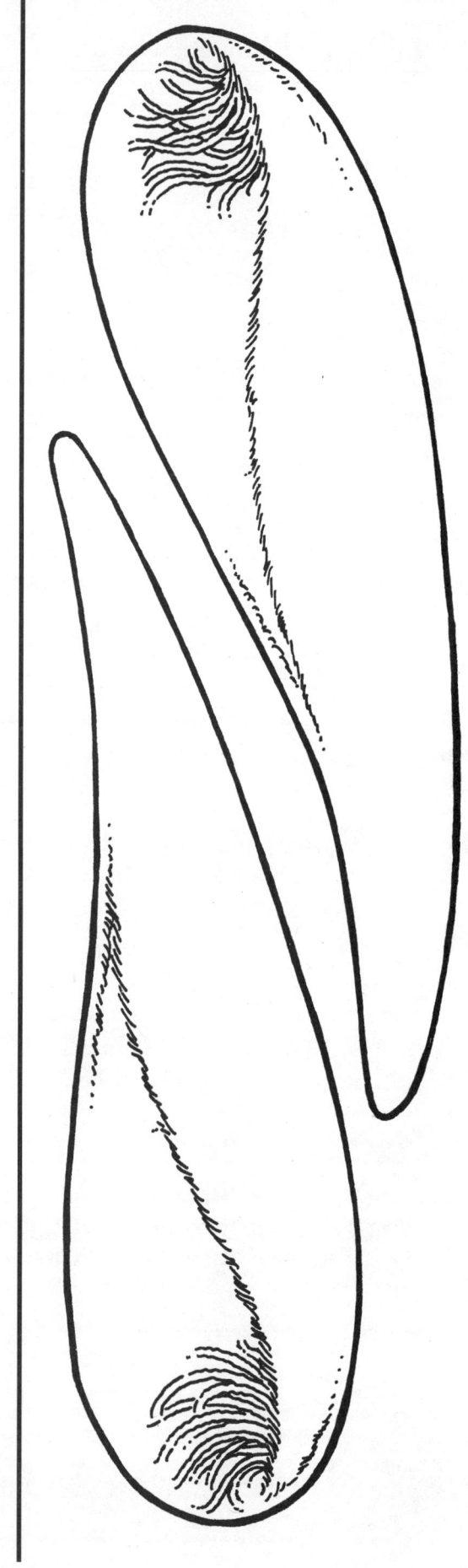

Reproducible 1A
Permission granted to photocopy for local church use. © 1999 Abingdon Press.

BibleZone®

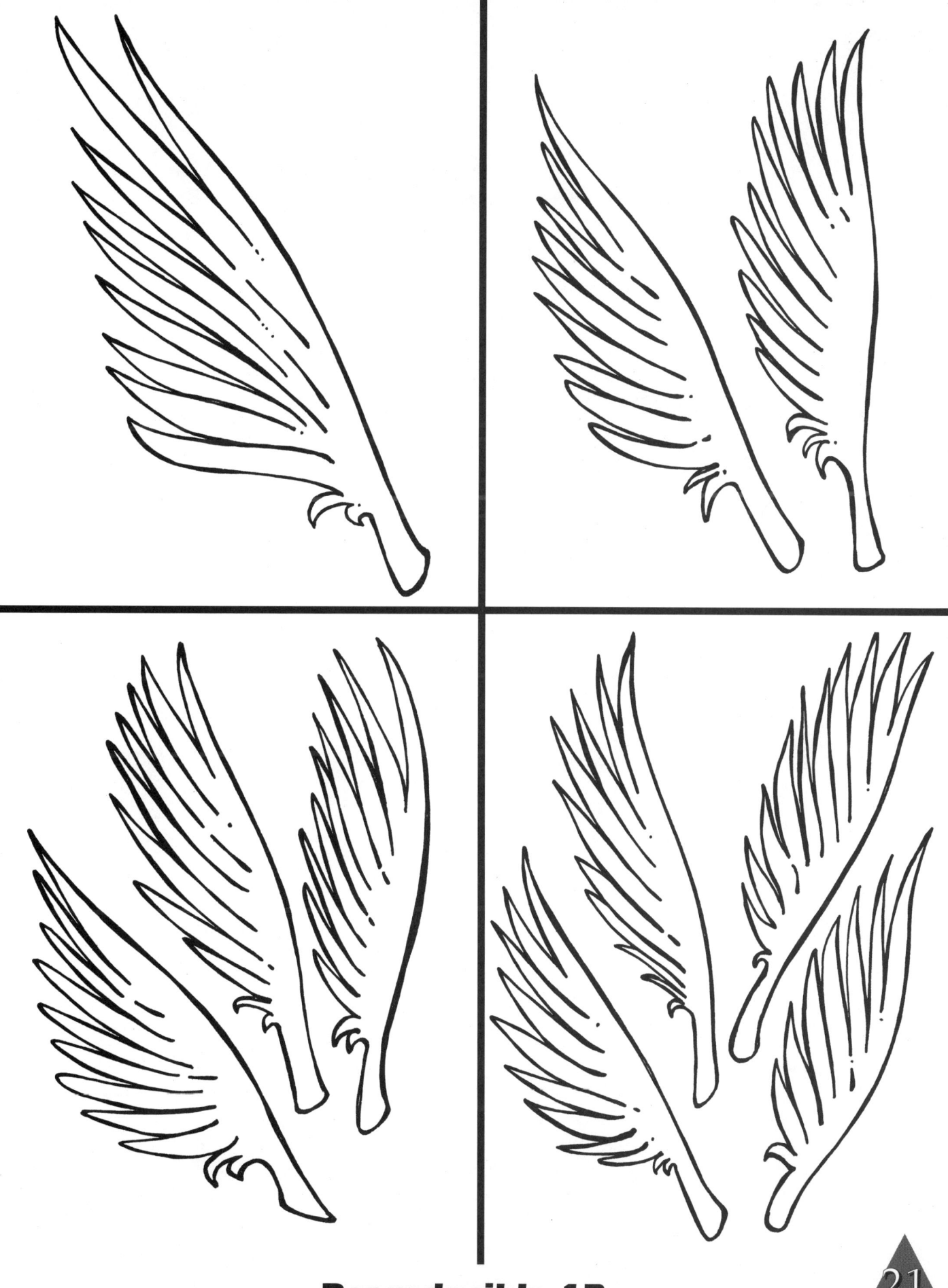

Reproducible 1B

2 BibleZone

Wash My Feet

Enter the Zone

Bible Verse
Love one another.
John 13:34

Bible Story
John 13:1-20, 34-35

The other three Gospels begin the story of the last time Jesus celebrated the Passover meal with his disciples by telling of the preparations made for the room and the meal. John begins by telling us that one of those preparations was overlooked—a basic demand of hospitality—the provision of a servant to wash the feet of the guests. In a hot and dusty land where everyone wore sandals, cool, fresh water and someone to help with the chore was a necessity for comfort. You may recall an earlier time when "a woman in the city" had performed a similar act by bathing Jesus' feet with her tears when his host had failed to provide water and a basin (Luke 7:36-50).

The Gospel of Luke tells of an argument at this last supper among the disciples as to which of them was to be regarded as the greatest (Luke 22:24-30). Perhaps this argument had been an ongoing one, in which case Jesus' act might be seen as a gentle reminder to them that ambition and rivalry would have no place in his kingdom.

Whatever the reason, the deed was sacramental as well as exemplary—Jesus set an example for the disciples, and their following this example would bring about a change in them that would make them fit for carrying on the work of the Lord. A service rendered to another is rendered to Jesus and through Jesus to God.

Your children will have had the experience of being hot and tired and being offered a cool drink, or a wet cloth to bathe their faces. They also are beginning to be aware of how their actions affect others, and they enjoy giving to others. Look for ways to reinforce these feelings in the classroom. Be sure to commend your children for their acts of kindness toward others that you observe in the classroom each Sunday morning.

We remember that Jesus loves us.

Scope the Zone

ZONE	TIME	SUPPLIES	ZILLIES
Zoom Into the Zone			
Clean Cool Color	10 minutes	Reproducible 2A, sponge, water, colored chalk; or crayons and markers	none
Feet Fun	5 minutes	none	none
BibleZone®			
Praise Parade	5 minutes	none	none
Wash My Feet	10 minutes	paint drop cloth, old shower curtains, or large towel for each child; Bible-times headdress; basin of warm, sudsy water, washcloth, towel	none
Bible Verse Buzz	5 minutes	Bible, BZ Bee	none
Sing!	5 minutes	cassette player	Cassette
LifeZone			
Love Prints	15 minutes	Reproducible 2B; paper towels, shallow tray, tempera paint, dish tub with soapy water, towels; newspaper or plastic; or sandal, crayons with papers removed	none
Bible Verse Beat	5 minutes	none	none
Puppet Prayers	5 minutes	none	lamb puppet

Zillies® are found in the **BibleZone® FUNspirational® Kit.**

Zoom Into the Zone

Choose one or more activities to catch your children's interest.

Supplies:
Reproducible 2A, sponge, water, colored chalk; or crayons or markers

Zillies®:
none

Clean Cool Color

Photocopy the picture of Jesus washing his friend's feet (**Reproducible 2A**) for each child. Give each child a picture.

Say: In Bible times people wore sandals without socks or went barefoot. When they walked on the dirt roads, their feet got dusty and dirty. Whenever they went inside a house to eat, they left their dusty sandals at the door. They wanted their feet to be clean and cool before they ate. Sometimes there were servants to wash their feet, and sometimes friends took turns washing each other's feet.

Wipe over each child's paper with a wet sponge. Let the children draw over the wet paper with colored chalk. Set the picture aside to dry completely. Or let the children decorate the pictures with crayons or markers.

Say: Today our Bible story is about the time when Jesus washed his friends' feet to show his love for his friends. He wanted his friends to remember him and to remember how much he loved them.

We remember that Jesus loves us.

Supplies:
none

Zillies®:
none

Feet Fun

Have the children move to an open area of the room. Say the following dialogue and have the children do the motions with you.

Say: In Bible times people wore sandals without socks or went barefoot. When they walked on the dirt roads, their feet got dusty and dirty. Let's pretend that we are Bible-times people. Let's put on our sandals. *(Pretend to put sandals on your feet.)* **Now let's take a walk.** *(Walk in place.)* **What a dusty road! My feet are already dirty.** *(Hold up one foot; hold up the other foot.)* **The road is hot. Let's hop on one foot.** *(Hop on one foot.)* **Now let's hop on the other foot.** *(Hop on other foot.)* **Whew, I'm tired.** *(Wipe hand over brow.)* **Let's sit down and rest.** *(Sit down.)* **Put your feet out in front of you.** *(Stretch legs out in front of your body.)* **Wiggle your toes.** *(Wiggle toes.)* **Stand up.** *(Stand up.)* **Stomp each foot once.** *(Stomp each foot.)* **Now let's have a praise parade.** *(Move into the "Praise Parade" activity on the next page.)*

Choose one or more activities to immerse your children in the Bible story.

Praise Parade

 se the following parade to lead your children around the room. Repeat the verses as necessary to lead the children to your story area.

Here comes the praise parade.
(March around the room.)
Here comes the praise parade.
Follow me and march, march, march.
Here comes the praise parade.

Praise God, praise God,
(Stop marching; hold arms above head and shake hands.)
Let's praise God for Jesus.
(Clap hands.)
Praise God, praise God,
(Hold arms above head and shake hands.)
Let's praise God today.
(Clap hands.)
Hurray!
(Hold arms up above head and jump.)

Here comes the praise parade.
(Stomp around the room.)
Here comes the praise parade.
Follow me and stomp, stomp, stomp.
Here comes the praise parade.

Praise God, praise God,
(Stop stomping; hold arms above head and shake hands.)
Let's praise God for Jesus.
(Clap hands.)
Praise God, praise God,
(Hold arms above head and shake hands.)
Let's praise God today.
(Clap hands.)
Hurray!
(Hold arms up above head and jump.)

Supplies:
none

Zillies®:
none

Bible Zone Story

Wash My Feet

by Sharilyn S. Adair

Cover the floor with plastic such as a paint drop cloth or one or more old shower curtains and/or provide a large towel for each child to sit on. Help the children remove their shoes and stockings and roll up any long pants legs. Wear a Bible-times headdress and have on hand a basin of warm sudsy water, a washcloth, and a towel.

In Bible times there were no cars to ride in. Everyone had to walk from place to place, or they had to ride donkeys. Most of their roads were made of dirt or sand. The weather was hot and dry, so people wore sandals without socks to keep their feet cool. When they walked on the dirt roads, the dust swirled up around them with every step, and their feet got dusty and dirty inside their sandals.

Whenever they went inside a house to eat, they left their dusty sandals at the door. Their tables were low to the floor, and they sat on mats on the floor to eat. They wanted their feet to be clean and cool before they ate. Sometimes there were servants to wash their feet, and sometimes friends took turns washing each other's feet.

Let's pretend that I am Jesus and that you are my friends. We have gathered together in a special room to have a meal. Let's sit down on mats around our pretend table here on the floor. There is no servant, and we don't remember whose turn it is to wash everyone's feet. None of you followers wants to be the foot washer, so everyone just sits with dirty feet. Pretend that your feet are hot and feel yucky. Then listen to what Jesus is thinking.

"I am so glad to be with my friends to eat this meal, but I am sad that nobody wants to wash the other people's feet. I know their feet are dirty and smelly; but if my friends loved one another the way I want them to, they would be glad to wash each other's feet anyway. I guess I will have to show each one how to be loving. *(Go to each child in turn, and call each by name.)*

"*(Child's name)*, would you like to put your feet in my basin and let me wash them? *(If some children do not want their feet washed, just pretend to swish over their feet with your washcloth.)* Ooh! Doesn't it feel good to have warm water on your feet?" *(After washing each child's feet, dry them with your towel. Continue until all the feet have been washed.)*

My friends, I want you to think about being kind and loving. If Jesus, your leader and teacher, loves you enough to wash your feet, you should love everyone else enough to wash his or her feet. Who would like to be the foot washer now?" *(If time permits, let the children take turns being the foot washer, or let pairs of children take turns washing each other's feet. When all have had a turn, put the water away. Dry each child's feet and help him or her put shoes and socks back on.)*

Zone In With BZ Bee

Bible Verse Buzz

Choose a child to hold the Bible open to John 13:34.

Say: Today our Bible story is about the time when Jesus washed his friends' feet to show his love for his friends. Jesus wanted his friends to remember that he loved them, and he wanted them to love one another.

Say the Bible verse, "Love one another" (John 13:34), for the children. Have the children say the Bible verse after you.

Turn your back to the children or hide your hands underneath a table or behind the **BibleZone® FUNspirational® Kit** lid as you place the **BZ Bee puppet** (see page 174) on your hand. Turn around or bring the puppet out where the children can see it.

Pretend to make the puppet talk. Change your voice for the puppet:

Bzzz. Bzzz. Bzzz. Hi, everybody! I'm BZ Bee. *Bzzz. Bzzz. Bzzz.* I like to taste fingers. Do you have fingers? Yum, yum, yum. Let me taste.

Go to each child. Encourage, but do not force, each child to hold up his or her fingers. Have BZ pretend to taste each child's fingers. Have BZ say things like:

Mmmm. Mmmm. You taste like honey.
Bzzz. Bzzz. You taste like strawberries.
Yumm. Yumm. You taste like blueberries.

After BZ has tasted each child's fingers, say:

Bzzz. Bzzz. Bzzz. I like to taste your fingers. They're yummy. *(Rub BZ's stomach.)*

Bzzz. Bzzz. Bzzz. I like something else even more than fingers.

I like the Bible. *Bzzz. Bzzz. Bzzz.* You heard a Bible story today. Who washed his friends' feet? *(Jesus)*

Bzzz. Bzzz. Bzzz. Jesus washed his friend's feet because he wanted his friends to remember him and to remember how much he loved them.

 **We remember that Jesus loves us.**

Bzzz. Bzzz. Bzzz. Let's say the Bible verse together.

"Love one another" (John 13:34).

Have the children repeat the Bible verse with BZ Bee.

Have BZ Bee say good-bye to the children. Put the puppet away.

Bible

Choose one or more activities to immerse your children in the Bible story.

Supplies:
cassette player

Zillies®:
Cassette

Sing!

Say: Today our Bible story is about the time when Jesus washed his friends' feet to show his love for his friends. Jesus wanted his friends to remember that he loved them, and he wanted them to love one another. We can remember that Jesus loves us. Jesus is our friend. Another name we call Jesus is Savior. Let's sing a song about Jesus, our friend and Savior.

Sing the song "He's My Savior" from the **Cassette.** The tune is "Are You Sleeping?"

He's My Savior

He's my Savior,
He's my Savior,
  Jesus Christ,
  Jesus Christ.

Sent from God in heaven,
Sent to earth to save us,

  He's my Friend.
  He's my Friend.

He's my Savior,
He's my Savior,
  Jesus Christ,
  Jesus Christ.

Sent from God in heaven,
Sent to earth to save us,

He's my Friend.
He's my Friend.

He's my Savior,
He's my Savior,
  Jesus Christ,
  Jesus Christ.

Sent from God in heaven,
Sent to earth to save us,

He's my Friend.
He's my Friend.

Writer: Steve Tanner
© 1998 New Spring Publishing/ASCAP
All Rights Reserved.
Used by permission of Brentwood-Benson Music Publishing, Inc.

From the Brentwood Music, Inc. recording *Kids Sing Praise vol.* 1.

Life Zone

Choose one or more activities to bring the Bible to life.

Love Prints

 hotocopy the Bible verse poster **(Reproducible 2B)** for each child.

Say: Today our Bible story is about the time when Jesus washed his friends' feet to show his love for his friends. Jesus wanted his friends to remember that he loved them, and he wanted them to love one another.

 **We remember that Jesus loves us.**

Give each child a Bible verse poster. Say the Bible verse, "Love one another" (John 13:34), for the children. Have the children repeat the verse. Let the children decorate their posters in one of the following ways:

Tiny footprints. Fold paper towels and place them in the bottom of a shallow tray. Pour tempera paint onto the paper towels to make a paint pad. Show the children how to make a fist with one of their hands. Press the side of the fist onto the paint pad and then onto the paper. The print from the side of the fist will look like a tiny footprint. The children may add toes to the footprint by making fingerprints. Have a dish tub of soapy water and towels available to wash and dry hands.

Sandal rubbings. Provide a sandal (adult or child-size). Remind the children that many Bible-times people wore sandals. When they walked along the dusty roads, their feet would get dirty inside their sandals. Place the sandal upside down on the table so that the sole of the sandal is facing up. Show the children how to place their papers over the sandal and then rub over their papers with the side of a crayon (with papers removed). The sole of the sandal will show through the rubbing.

Footprints. Cover the floor with newspapers or with a sheet of plastic. Fold paper towels and place them in the bottom of a shallow tray. Pour tempera paint onto the paper towels to make a paint pad. Place a tub of soapy water and some towels next to the paint pad. Place the child's Bible verse poster on the newspaper or plastic. Help each child remove his or her shoes and socks. Have each child place a foot onto the paint pad and then press her or his foot onto the poster. Immediately help the child wash his or her foot in the tub of soapy water and dry it with a towel.

Note: This activity needs adult supervision at all times. Plan to have the children make their footprints one at a time.

Supplies:
Reproducible 2B; paper towels, shallow tray, tempera paint, dish tub with soapy water, towels; or sandal, crayons with papers removed; or newspaper or plastic, paper towels, shallow tray, tempera paint, dish tub, soapy water, towels

Zillies®:
none

Life

Choose one or more activities to bring the Bible to life.

Supplies:
none

Zillies®:
none

Bible Verse Beat

ave the children stand in an open area of the room. Enjoy using the following action poem with the children to help them learn the Bible verse, "Love one another" (John 13:34).

Clap your hands.
(Clap hands as you say each word.)
Stomp your feet.
(Stomp feet as you say each word.)
Let's all do the Bible verse beat!
(Hold hands above head and shake fingers; turn around.)

Clap, clap, clap.
(Clap hands as you say each word.)
Stomp, stomp, stomp.
(Stomp feet as you say each word.)
Love one another!
(Hold hands above head and shake fingers; turn around.)

Supplies:
none

Zillies®:
lamb puppet

Puppet Prayers

ave the children sit down. Show the children the **lamb puppet**.

Say: This is my puppet, Lambkins. What kind of animal is Lambkins? *(lamb, sheep)* **Lambs help us remember the new life that God plans for us in God's world. Lambs can also help us remember that Jesus taught us about new life. Lambkins wants to help us praise God for Jesus and new life.**

Hold up the lamb puppet and sing the following song to the tune of "Are You Sleeping?" Pretend that the puppet is singing one line, and have the children sing the repeating line after the puppet.

> Here is Lambkins,
> **Here is Lambkins,**
> Come to say,
> **Come to say,**
> "Let's praise God for Jesus
> **"Let's praise God for Jesus**
> As we pray."
> **As we pray."**

Pray: Thank you, God, for Jesus. Thank you, God, for new life. Amen.

Photocopy the **HomeZone®** newsletter to send home to parents.

Home Zone For Parents

Bible Verse
Love one another. John 13:34

Bible Story
John 13:1-20, 34-35

Wash My Feet

Today's Bible story centers around the time when Jesus washed the disciples' feet. Jesus wanted his disciples to know that he loved them, and he wanted them to show love to others. He set an example for the disciples by doing the work usually done by a servant.

Foot Washing

Talk with your child about today's Bible story. Tell your child that people in Bible times wore sandals without socks or went barefoot. When they walked on the dirt roads, their feet got dusty and dirty. Whenever they went inside a house to eat, they left their dusty sandals at the door. They wanted their feet to be clean and cool before they ate. Sometimes there were servants to wash their feet, and sometimes friends took turns washing each other's feet. Jesus washed his friend's feet to show his love for his friends. Jesus wanted his friends to remember that he loved them, and he wanted them to love one another.

Pour water into a dish tub. Use the water, a washcloth, and a towel to wash your child's feet. Let your child wash your feet.

We remember that Jesus loves us.

Reproducible 2A

Permission granted to photocopy for local church use. © 1999 Abingdon Press.

3 Bible

Remember Me

Enter the

Bible Verse
Do this in memory of me.
Luke 22:19, *Good News Bible*

Bible Story
Luke 22:7-20

Jesus and his friends came to Jerusalem to celebrate the Passover. During this meal the Jewish people remember how Moses led the Hebrew people out of slavery in Egypt. Since Passover is a family celebration, as righteous Jews, Jesus and his friends and all their families would have made the trip to Jerusalem. Several families could share Passover together, but they had to band together into identifiable groups. Jesus would have sat at the table with his twelve apostles. He would have served as head of the family group, saying the special blessings designated to the father. But Jesus had another message to deliver on this special evening.

Each food of the Passover seder had a special significance that would remind the people of the story of Moses. Jesus, as a good teacher, used these familiar items of Passover—the bread and the wine—to show what was about to happen to him and what these events would mean to the disciples. Through this meal, known today as the Last Supper, Jesus gave his disciples a new way to remember him.

Preschool children probably will have difficulty understanding abstract concepts such as the bread and the cup symbolizing the body and blood of Jesus. In fact, this symbolism can even be frightening for young children. Instead, help your children understand Communion as a way to remember that Jesus loves us.

Note: Talk with your pastor and your parents if you want to serve Holy Communion as part of this lesson.

We remember that Jesus loves us.

Scope the Zone

ZONE	TIME	SUPPLIES	ZILLIES
Zoom Into the Zone			
Concentrate!	10 minutes	Reproducible 3A, scissors	none
What's Missing?	10 minutes	Reproducible 3A, scissors	none
BibleZone			
Praise Parade	5 minutes	none	none
Remember Me	10 minutes	Reproducible 3B, jar of water, uncut hoagie roll, glass or grape juice or red punch, plate, cup or chalice your church uses for Communion	none
Bible Verse Buzz	5 minutes	Bible, BZ Bee	none
Sing!	5 minutes	cassette player	Cassette
LifeZone			
Great Grapes	10 minutes	Reproducible 3A, scissors; construction paper; green crayons; paper towels; shallow tray; purple tempera paint; newspapers; smocks; milk or juice jug lids, empty thread spools, film canisters, or cardboard rolls and tape	none
Taste Grapes	10 minutes	napkins, grapes	none
Bible Verse Songfest	5 minutes	none	none
Puppet Prayers	5 minutes	none	lamb puppet

Zillies® are found in the **BibleZone® FUNspirational® Kit.**

Zoom Into the Zone

Choose one or more activities to catch your children's interest.

Supplies:
Reproducible 3A, scissors

Zillies®:
none

Concentrate!

Photocopy and cut apart at least two sets of the Communion picture cards **(Reproducible 3A)**. Place the cards face down on the table or rug. Have a child turn over one picture. Then have the child turn over one more picture to try to match the first picture. Help the children identify the pictures as they are turned over. If the pictures match, leave both pictures face up. If the pictures do not match, turn the pictures face down again. Let the children take turns turning over the cards until all the matches are found.

Say: You had to remember where the pictures were in order to play this game. Today our Bible story is about the time when Jesus wanted his friends to remember how much he loved them. Jesus shared a special meal with his friends. Jesus and his friends ate bread and drank juice from a cup at the special meal. Our church has a special meal called Communion, where we eat bread and drink juice. At Communion we remember Jesus.

We remember that Jesus loves us.

Supplies:
Reproducible 3A, scissors

Zillies®:
none

What's Missing?

Photocopy and cut apart one set of the Communion pictures **(Reproducible 3A)**. Place the pictures face up on the table or rug. Help the children identify each picture. Have the children cover their eyes with their hands. Take one picture away from the set and hide it behind your back. Have the children uncover their eyes. Encourage the children to remember what picture is missing. When the children have named the picture, show the children the picture and place it back on the table or rug. Repeat the game and remove a different picture each time.

Say: You had to remember all the pictures in order to play this game. Today our Bible story is about the time when Jesus wanted his friends to remember how much he loved them. Jesus shared a special meal with his friends. Jesus and his friends ate bread and drank juice from a cup at the special meal. Our church has a special meal called Communion where we eat bread and drink juice. At Communion we remember that Jesus loves us.

Bible

Choose one or more activities to immerse your children in the Bible story.

Praise Parade

 Use the following parade to lead your children around the room. Repeat the verses as necessary to lead the children to your story area.

Here comes the praise parade.
(March around the room.)
Here comes the praise parade.
Follow me and march, march, march.
Here comes the praise parade.

Praise God, praise God,
(Stop marching; hold arms above head and shake hands.)
Let's praise God for Jesus.
(Clap hands.)
Praise God, praise God,
(Hold arms above head and shake hands.)
Let's praise God today.
(Clap hands.)
Hurray!
(Hold arms up above head and jump.)

Here comes the praise parade.
(Stomp around the room.)
Here comes the praise parade.
Follow me and stomp, stomp, stomp.
Here comes the praise parade.

Praise God, praise God,
(Stop stomping; hold arms above head and shake hands.)
Let's praise God for Jesus.
(Clap hands.)
Praise God, praise God,
(Hold arms above head and shake hands.)
Let's praise God today.
(Clap hands.)
Hurray!
(Hold arms up above head and jump.)

Supplies:
none

Zillies®:
none

Bible Zone Story

Remember Me

by Sharilyn S. Adair

Photocopy and cut apart the jar, bread, cup, and room pictures **(Reproducible 3B)**. *Gather a jar of water, an uncut hoagie roll, a glass of grape juice or red punch, and a plate and one of the cups or the chalice your church uses for Communion. Invite the children to sit down in a circle in your story area.*

Say: *I have some things for you to see and feel that are in today's story. When I come to the part of the story where each thing is mentioned, I will let you see or feel it.*

"Peter! John!" said Jesus. "I want you to go fix a Passover meal for us to eat." The Passover meal was a special celebration meal. Peter and John were surprised. "Where do you want us to fix it?" they asked.

"Go into the city," Jesus said. "You will see a man carrying a jar of water. *(Pass around a small jar of water. Show the children the picture of a Bible-times jar.)* Follow him to a house. When you go into the house, say to the owner, 'Our teacher wants to know where the room is where he can eat the Passover meal with his disciples.' The man will show you a large room upstairs that already has a table and seats. *(Show the children the picture of the Upper Room.)* Fix our meal there." So Peter and John did as they were asked.

When it was time for the meal, Jesus and all of the disciples gathered around the table. "Listen, my friends," said Jesus. "I have been looking forward to eating this meal with you. It is a special meal. I will not eat another meal like this."

First Jesus took a loaf of bread and said a thank-you prayer for the bread. *(Show the children the bread picture. Show a loaf of unsliced bread or a hoagie roll.)* He told his disciples, "Whenever you eat bread like this from now on, I want you to remember me." Then he broke the bread. *(Break the bread.)*

Then Jesus took a cup of juice in his hands and said a thank-you prayer for the wine. *(Show the children the picture of the cup. Show a glass with grape juice or red punch in it.)* He told his followers, "Whenever you drink juice like this from now on, I want you to remember me."

Jesus' friends were happy to be eating the Passover meal with him. Ever after that, they remembered Jesus whenever they ate a special meal of bread and juice. We remember Jesus today when we have a special time in church called Communion. We eat bread and drink grape juice to remember how much Jesus loves us. *(Show the plate and one of the cups or the chalice your church uses for Communion. Ask if any of the children have seen or taken Communion in your church. Talk with them about your service and about how it is a way your church remembers Jesus.)*

Zone In With BZ Bee

Bible Verse Buzz

hoose a child to hold the Bible open to Luke 22:19.

Say: Today our Bible story is about the time when Jesus shared a special meal with his friends. Jesus asked his friends to remember him each time they ate together. Jesus said, "Do this in memory of me" (Luke 22:19, *Good News Bible*).

Say the Bible verse, "Do this in memory of me" (Luke 22:19, *Good News Bible*), for the children. Have the children say the Bible verse after you.

Turn your back to the children or hide your hands underneath a table or behind the **BibleZone® FUNspirational® Kit** lid as you place the **BZ Bee puppet** (see page 174) on your hand. Turn around or bring the puppet out where the children can see it.

Pretend to make the puppet talk. Change your voice for the puppet:

Bzzz. Bzzz. Bzzz. Hi, everybody! I'm BZ Bee. *Bzzz. Bzzz. Bzzz.* I like to taste fingers. Do you have fingers? Yum, yum, yum. Let me taste.

Go to each child. Encourage, but do not force, each child to hold up his or her fingers. Have BZ pretend to taste each child's fingers. Have BZ say things like:

Mmmm. Mmmm. You taste like honey.
Bzzz. Bzzz. You taste like strawberries.
Yumm. Yumm. You taste like blueberries.

After BZ has tasted each child's fingers, say:

Bzzz. Bzzz. Bzzz. I like to taste your fingers. They're yummy. *(Rub BZ's stomach.)*

Bzzz. Bzzz. Bzzz. I like something else even more than fingers.

I like the Bible. *Bzzz. Bzzz. Bzzz.* You heard a Bible story today. Who shared a special meal with his friends? *(Jesus)* What did they eat at the meal? *(bread)* What did they drink at the meal? *(wine, grape juice)*

Bzzz. Bzzz. Bzzz. When Jesus shared a special meal with his friends, he asked his friends to remember him and to remember how much he loved them.

 **We remember that Jesus loves us.**

Bzzz. Bzzz. Bzzz. Let's say the Bible verse together.

"Do this in memory of me" (Luke 22:19, *Good News Bible*).

Have the children repeat the Bible verse with BZ Bee. Have BZ Bee say good-bye to the children. Put the puppet away.

Bible

Choose one or more activities to immerse your children in the Bible story.

Supplies:
cassette player

Zillies®:
Cassette

Sing!

Say: Today our Bible story is about the time when Jesus shared a special meal with his friends. Jesus asked his friends to remember him each time they ate together. Jesus wanted his friends to remember that he loved them. We can remember that Jesus loves us. Jesus is our friend. Another name we call Jesus is Savior. Let's sing a song about Jesus, our friend and Savior.

Sing the song "He's My Savior" from the **Cassette**. The tune is "Are You Sleeping?"

He's My Savior

He's my Savior,
He's my Savior,
  Jesus Christ,
  Jesus Christ.

Sent from God in heaven,
Sent to earth to save us,

  He's my Friend.
  He's my Friend.

He's my Savior,
He's my Savior,
  Jesus Christ,
  Jesus Christ.

Sent from God in heaven,
Sent to earth to save us,

He's my Friend.
He's my Friend.

He's my Savior,
He's my Savior,
  Jesus Christ,
  Jesus Christ.

Sent from God in heaven,
Sent to earth to save us,

He's my Friend.
He's my Friend.

Writer: Steve Tanner
© 1998 New Spring Publishing/ASCAP
All Rights Reserved.
Used by permission of Brentwood-Benson Music Publishing, Inc.

From the Brentwood Music, Inc. recording *Kids Sing Praise vol. 1*.

Choose one or more activities to bring the Bible to life.

Great Grapes

Photocopy and cut out the grape picture **(Reproducible 3A)**. Show the picture to the children.

Say: Jesus shared a special meal with his friends. Jesus and his friends ate bread and drank juice from a cup at the special meal. The juice Jesus and his friends drank was made from grapes. Let's make pictures of grapes.

Cover the work area with newspapers and have the children wear smocks to protect their clothing. Place paper towels into a shallow tray. Pour purple tempera paint onto the towels to make a paint pad.

Provide milk jug or juice jug lids, empty thread spools, film canisters, or cardboard rolls. If you use cardboard rolls, tape three cardboard rolls together. (These may be three toilet paper rolls or a paper towel roll cut into three pieces.) Give each child a piece of construction paper. Show the children how to press the ends of the items onto the paint pad and then onto their papers to make clusters of grapes. Let the children add a stem or leaves with a green crayon. Set the pictures aside to dry and have the children wash their hands.

Say: We drink grape juice at a special meal called Communion. When we drink the grape juice at Communion, we can remember that Jesus loves us.

Supplies:
Reproducible 3A, scissors; construction paper; green crayons; paper towels; shallow tray; purple tempera paint; newspapers; smocks; milk or juice jug lids, empty thread spools, film canisters, or cardboard rolls and tape

Zillies®:
none

Taste Grapes

Have the children sit down at the table. Choose a child to hand out napkins. Show the children the grapes you have provided.

Say: Jesus shared a special meal with his friends. Jesus and his friends ate bread and drank juice from a cup at the special meal. The juice Jesus and his friends drank was made from grapes. Let's taste grapes.

Let the children share the grapes.

Pray: Thank you, God, for Jesus. Thank you, God for grapes.

Supplies:
napkins, grapes

Zillies®:
none

Life Zone

Choose one or more activities to bring the Bible to life.

Supplies:
none

Zillies®:
none

Bible Verse Songfest

Say: Today our Bible story is about the time when Jesus shared a special meal with his friends. Jesus asked his friends to remember him each time they ate together. Jesus said, "Do this in memory of me" (Luke 22:19, *Good News Bible*).

Sing the Bible verse with the children to the tune of "The Farmer in the Dell."

"Do this in memory of me."
"Do this in memory of me."
We remember Jesus said:
"Do this in memory of me."

Supplies:
none

Zillies®:
lamb puppet

Puppet Prayers

Have the children sit down. Show the children the **lamb puppet**.

Say: This is my puppet, Lambkins. What kind of animal is Lambkins? *(lamb, sheep)* **Lambs help us remember the new life God plans for us in God's world. Lambs can also help us remember that Jesus taught us about new life. Lambkins wants to help us praise God for Jesus and for new life.**

Hold up the lamb puppet and sing the following song to the tune of "Are You Sleeping?" Pretend that the puppet is singing one line, and have the children sing the repeating line after the puppet.

Here is Lambkins,
Here is Lambkins,
Come to say,
Come to say,
"Let's praise God for Jesus
"Let's praise God for Jesus
As we pray."
As we pray."

Pray: Thank you, God, for Jesus. Thank you, God, for new life. Amen.

Photocopy the **HomeZone®** newsletter to send home to parents.

Home Zone For Parents

Bible Verse
Do this in memory of me.
Luke 22:19, Good News Bible

Bible Story
Luke 22:7-20

Remember Me

Today your child heard the story of when Jesus shared the Passover meal with his disciples. Through this meal, the Last Supper, Jesus gave his disciples a new way to remember him.

Preschool children may have difficulty understanding abstract concepts such as the bread and the cup symbolizing the body and blood of Jesus. In fact, this symbolism can even be frightening for young children. Help your child understand Communion as a way to remember that Jesus loves us.

Love Pretzels

Make heart-shaped pretzels with your child. Thaw frozen bread or use the canned, refrigerated bread sticks. Give your child a section of bread dough or a bread dough stick. Show your child how to roll the dough into a snake-like shape. Let your child form the bread roll into a heart shape. Place the heart shape on a baking tray. Brush the top of the bread with melted butter. Sprinkle coarse salt over the top. Bake at 350 degrees for ten to twelve minutes.

Remind your child that Jesus and his friends shared a special meal. They ate bread and drank juice at the meal. Jesus asked his friends to remember how much he loved them. We remember that Jesus loves us.

We remember that Jesus loves us.

PRESCHOOL 7   Permission granted to photocopy for local church use. © 1999 Abingdon Press.

Reproducible 3A

Permission granted to photocopy for local church use. © 1999 Abingdon Press.

BibleZone®

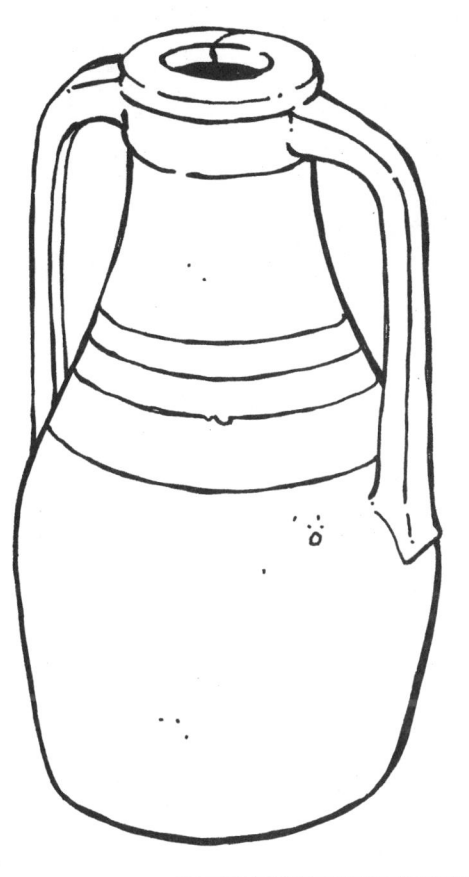

PRESCHOOL 7

Reproducible 3B

Permission granted to photocopy for local church use. © 1999 Abingdon Press.

45

4 Bible

Jesus Lives!

Enter the

Bible Verse
See, everything has become new!
2 Corinthians 5:17

Bible Story
Matthew 28:1–7

The story of Jesus' resurrection is the heart and soul of the Christian faith: Jesus IS alive! Because Jesus lives, we have the new life God promised.

When Jesus was crucified, the priests heard the rumors of Jesus' claim to rise from the dead on the third day. They did not want the disciples to sneak inside the tomb and steal the body so that the disciples could claim that Jesus had risen. The priests stationed guards around the tomb and had the tomb sealed. The Jewish sabbath began on that same Friday at sunset and continued through sunset on Saturday. During that time no work could be done, including preparing a body for proper burial. So on the morning after the sabbath, some of Jesus' women friends came to the tomb to give the body a proper burial with oils and spices.

When the women arrived at the tomb, it was empty. Between the message of the angel and the meetings with Jesus himself, the company of believers who had followed Jesus came to the wonderful realization that Jesus was indeed alive.

Children may have questions about the resurrection. Answer them as simply and as honestly as possible. As adults we still don't have all the answers. It's perfectly acceptable to say, "I don't know." What we do know is that with God, anything is possible.

Today is a time to celebrate new life in all its forms. Jesus is alive! Create a celebratory mood in your class. Help your children understand that God gave Jesus new life and that, through Jesus, we also have new life.

Jesus gives new life.

Scope the Zone

ZONE	TIME	SUPPLIES	ZILLIES®
Zoom Into the Zone			
Tomb Turnaround	10 minutes	Reproducible 4A, crayons or markers; tape, glue, or stapler and staples	none
From Sad to Happy	5 minutes	tomb picture (Reproducible 4A)	none
BibleZone®			
Praise Parade	5 minutes	none	none
Jesus Lives!	10 minutes	tomb picture (Reproducible 4A)	rock ball
Bible Verse Buzz	5 minutes	Bible, BZ Bee	none
Sing!	5 minutes	cassette player	Cassette
LifeZone			
Butterflies Flutterby	15 minutes	Reproducible 4B, crayons or markers, scissors, tape or glue	green crepe paper
Bible Verse Songfest	5 minutes	none	none
Puppet Prayers	5 minutes	none	lamb puppet

Zillies® are found in the **BibleZone® FUNspirational® Kit.**

Zoom Into the Zone

Choose one or more activities to catch your children's interest.

Supplies:
Reproducible 4A, crayons or markers; tape, glue, or stapler and staples

Zillies®:
none

Tomb Turnaround

hotocopy one copy of the tomb (**Reproducible 4A**). Show the picture to the children.

Say: Today our Bible story is very special. Jesus died and was buried in a tomb. The tomb was like a cave. Jesus' body was put in the tomb, and a big rock was rolled in front of the door. *(Show the children the picture of the tomb with the rock in front of the opening, Reproducible 4A.)* **Two women came to see the tomb. They were sad because their friend Jesus was dead. But when they saw the tomb, they were surprised! The rock was rolled away from the door.** *(Show the children the picture of the tomb with the rock rolled away from the opening, Reproducible 4A.)* **They looked inside the tomb. Jesus was not there! The women were happy. They knew Jesus was alive! They knew Jesus gives new life.**

 **Jesus gives new life.**

Let the children decorate the tomb pictures with crayons or markers. Fold the picture on the dotted line. Tape, glue, or staple the sides of the picture together. Place your hand in the bottom opening of the picture. Turn the picture one way to show the tomb with the rock in front of the opening. Turn the picture around to show the tomb with the rock rolled away.

Supplies:
tomb picture (Reproducible 4A)

Zillies®:
none

From Sad to Happy

ave the children move to an open area of the room.

Say: Let's pretend that we are the women going to see the tomb. *(Show the children the picture of the tomb with the rock in front of the opening, Reproducible 4A.)* **We are feeling very sad. Show me how you walk when you are feeling sad.** *(Encourage the children to walk around the room.)* **Wait!** *(Have the children stop walking.)* **Look at the tomb!** *(Show the children the picture of the tomb with the rock rolled away, Reproducible 4A.)* **The rock has been rolled away! Let's look inside the tomb.** *(Hold hand above eyes and pretend to peer inside the tomb.)* **Jesus is not here! Jesus is alive! Now we are happy. Let's jump up and down with joy.** *(Jump up and down.)* **Let's run and tell Jesus' friends.** *(Run in place.)* **Jesus is alive!**

# Bible

Choose one or more activities to immerse your children in the Bible story.

Praise Parade

se the following parade to lead your children around the room. Repeat the verses as necessary to lead the children to your story area.

Here comes the praise parade.
(March around the room.)
Here comes the praise parade.
Follow me and march, march, march.
Here comes the praise parade.

Praise God, praise God,
(Stop marching; hold arms above head and shake hands.)
Let's praise God for Jesus.
(Clap hands.)
Praise God, praise God,
(Hold arms above head and shake hands.)
Let's praise God today.
(Clap hands.)
Hurray!
(Hold arms up above head and jump.)

Here comes the praise parade.
(Stomp around the room.)
Here comes the praise parade.
Follow me and stomp, stomp, stomp.
Here comes the praise parade.

Praise God, praise God,
(Stop stomping; hold arms above head and shake hands.)
Let's praise God for Jesus.
(Clap hands.)
Praise God, praise God,
(Hold arms above head and shake hands.)
Let's praise God today.
(Clap hands.)
Hurray!
(Hold arms up above head and jump.)

Supplies:
none

Zillies®:
none

Bible Zone Story

Jesus Lives!

by Sharilyn S. Adair

ave the children sit in the circle on the floor. Have the **rock ball** and the picture of the tomb **(Reproducible 4A)** ready to show to the children.

Say: Today's story has a big rock in it. The rock makes a door for a kind of cave called a tomb, a place where someone who is dead can be buried. (Show the children the picture of the tomb with the stone rolled in front of the opening.) **In order for anyone to get into the tomb, the big rock must be rolled away from the door.** (Show the children the picture of the tomb with the stone rolled away from the opening.) **I will roll this rock** (Show the children the rock ball.) **to (name a child) and start the story. The first time I say the word** rolled, **(child's name) must roll the rock to someone else. That person must wait until I say "roll" or "rolled" again and must roll the rock to another person who has not had the rock yet. Every time I say "roll" or "rolled," whoever has the rock must roll it to someone else.**

Very early one morning, just as the sun was coming up, two women named Mary were walking and talking. Their friend Jesus had died, and they were going to see his tomb. One Mary's name was Mary Magdalene. Mary Magdalene said to the other Mary, "I hope we can go inside the tomb, but I think a big rock has been **rolled** in front of the door."

"Oh, dear!" said the other Mary. "Is it a very big rock? Can we **roll** it away by ourselves?"

"I think it might be too heavy for us to **roll** away," said Mary Magdalene. "Some soldiers had to push and push to **roll** it in front of the door. I don't think we can **roll** it all by ourselves."

The two Marys wondered who could **roll** the rock away from the door. They really wanted to go inside, but they thought no one would be there to help **roll** the rock away.

What a surprise! When Mary Magdalene and the other Mary got to the tomb, they did not have to **roll** the rock at all. An angel came and **rolled** it away from the door. Then the angel sat on top of the rock that he had **rolled** away.

"Do not be afraid," said the angel. "Your friend Jesus is not here. He is alive. Come in and see the place where he was." So the two Marys went through the open doorway where the rock had been **rolled** away. What the angel said was true. Jesus was not there!

"Go quickly and tell all the other followers," the angel said. "Jesus is not dead anymore. He is going to Galilee. They can meet him there."

Mary Magdalene and the other Mary were a little bit afraid but also very excited and happy. They ran out of the tomb past the rock that had been **rolled** away. They could hardly wait to tell the other followers, "Jesus is alive!"

In With BZ Bee

Bible Verse Buzz

hoose a child to hold the Bible open to 2 Corinthians 5:17.

Say: Jesus died and was buried in a tomb. Two of Jesus' friends went to the tomb, but Jesus was not in the tomb. Jesus was alive! Today we remember that Jesus brings new life.

Say the Bible verse, "See, everything has become new!" (2 Corinthians 5:17), for the children. Have the children say the Bible verse after you.

Turn your back to the children or hide your hands underneath a table or behind the **BibleZone® FUNspirational® Kit** lid as you place the **BZ Bee puppet** (see page 174) on your hand. Turn around or bring the puppet out where the children can see it.

Pretend to make the puppet talk. Change your voice for the puppet:

Bzzz. Bzzz. Bzzz. Hi, everybody! I'm BZ Bee. Bzzz. Bzzz. Bzzz. I like to taste fingers. Do you have fingers? Yum, yum, yum. Let me taste.

Go to each child. Encourage, but do not force, each child to hold up his or her fingers. Have BZ pretend to taste each child's fingers. Have BZ say things like:

Mmmm. Mmmm. You taste like honey. Bzzz. Bzzz. You taste like strawberries. Yumm. Yumm. You taste like blueberries.

After BZ has tasted each child's fingers, say:

Bzzz. Bzzz. Bzzz. I like to taste your fingers. They're yummy. (Rub BZ's stomach.)

Bzzz. Bzzz. Bzzz. I like something else even more than fingers.

I like the Bible. *Bzzz. Bzzz. Bzzz.* You heard a Bible story today. Who went to the tomb? *(Mary Magdalene and the other Mary; two of Jesus' friends)* Where was the big rock that covered the door of the tomb? *(rolled away)* Did the women find Jesus in the tomb? *(No)*

Bzzz. Bzzz. Bzzz. Jesus is alive!

 **Jesus gives new life.**

Bzzz. Bzzz. Bzzz. Let's say the Bible verse together.

"See, everything has become new!" (2 Corinthians 5:17).

Have the children repeat the Bible verse with BZ Bee. Have BZ Bee say good-bye to the children. Put the puppet away.

Choose one or more activities to immerse your children in the Bible story.

Supplies:
cassette player

Zillies®:
Cassette

Sing!

ay: Jesus died and was buried in a tomb. Two of Jesus' friends went to the tomb, but Jesus was not in the tomb. Jesus was alive!

Sing the song "Alive, Alive" from the **Cassette.**

Alive, Alive

Alive, alive,
Alive forevermore;
My Jesus is alive,
Alive forevermore.
Alive, alive,
Alive forevermore;
My Jesus is alive.

Sing Hallelujah!
Sing Hallelujah!
My Jesus is alive forevermore.
Sing Hallelujah!
Sing Hallelujah!
My Jesus is alive!

Alive, alive,
Alive forevermore;
My Jesus is alive,
Alive forevermore.
Alive, alive,
Alive forevermore;
My Jesus is alive.

Sing Hallelujah!
Sing Hallelujah!
My Jesus is alive forevermore.
Sing Hallelujah!
Sing Hallelujah!
My Jesus is alive!
My Jesus is alive!

© 1986 New Spring Publishing/ASCAP
All Rights Reserved.
Used by Permission of Brentwood-Benson Music Publishing, Inc.

From the Brentwood Music, Inc. recording *Kids Sing Praise vol. 2.*

Choose one or more activities to bring the Bible to life.

Butterflies Flutterby

Supplies:
Reproducible 4B, crayons or markers, scissors, tape or glue

Zillies®:
green crepe paper

hotocopy and cut apart the butterfly strips **(Reproducible 4B)** for each child. Give each child a strip.

Say: Butterflies can help us remember that God plans for new life. The butterfly begins life as a tiny egg. The egg hatches into a caterpillar. The caterpillar eats and eats and eats until the time is ready. Then it spins a cocoon and sleeps. While the caterpillar sleeps, its body changes into a new creature. It changes into a butterfly. When we see butterflies, we can remember our Bible verse, "See, everything has become new!" (2 Corinthians 5:17), and we can remember Jesus.

 **Jesus gives new life.**

Let the children decorate the butterflies with crayons or markers. Show the children how to glue or tape the ends of each strip together to make a wrist band. Let the children glue or tape strips of **green crepe paper** to their wrist bands. Encourage the children to wear the wrist bands.

Read the litany printed below. Have the children wave their arms up and down like butterfly wings each time you say the refrain.

Have you heard the good news?

**Butterflies of every color,
Yellow, orange, and blue,
Remind us all that Jesus lives
And everything is new!**

Jesus is not dead.

**Butterflies of every color,
Yellow, orange, and blue,
Remind us all that Jesus lives
And everything is new!**

Jesus is alive!

**Butterflies of every color,
Yellow, orange, and blue,
Remind us all that Jesus lives
And everything is new!**

See, everything has become new!

**Butterflies of every color,
Yellow, orange, and blue,
Remind us all that Jesus lives
And everything is new!**

Life

Choose one or more activities to bring the Bible to life.

Supplies:
none

Zillies®:
none

Bible Verse Songfest

Say: Jesus died and was buried in a tomb. Two of Jesus' friends went to the tomb, but Jesus was not in the tomb. Jesus was alive! Today we remember that Jesus brings new life.

Sing the Bible verse with the children to the tune of "The Farmer in the Dell."

"See, everything has become new."
"See, everything has become new."
Jesus gives us all new life.
"See, everything has become new."

Supplies:
none

Zillies®:
lamb puppet

Puppet Prayers

Have the children sit down. Show the children the **lamb puppet**.

Say: This is my puppet, Lambkins. What kind of animal is Lambkins? *(lamb, sheep)* Lambs help us remember the new life God plans for us in God's world. Lambs also can help us remember that Jesus taught us about new life. Lambkins wants to help us praise God for Jesus and for new life.

Hold up the lamb puppet and sing the following song to the tune of "Are You Sleeping?" Pretend that the puppet is singing one line, and have the children sing the repeating line after the puppet.

Here is Lambkins,
Here is Lambkins,
Come to say,
Come to say,
"Let's praise God for Jesus
"Let's praise God for Jesus
As we pray."
As we pray."

Pray: Thank you, God, for Jesus. Thank you, God, for new life. Amen.

Photocopy the **HomeZone®** newsletter to send home to parents.

Home Zone For Parents

Bible Verse
See, everything has become new!
2 Corinthians 5:17

Bible Story
Matthew 28:1–7

Jesus Lives!

The story of Jesus' resurrection is the heart and soul of the Christian faith: Jesus IS alive! Because Jesus lives, we have the new life God promised.

Your child may have questions about the resurrection. Answer them as simply and as honestly as possible. As adults we still don't have all the answers. It's perfectly acceptable to say, "I don't know." What we do know is that with God, anything is possible.

Today is a time to celebrate new life in all its forms. Jesus is alive! Help your child understand that God gave Jesus new life and that, through Jesus, we also have new life.

Sandwichflies

Tell your child that butterflies can help us remember that God plans for new life. The butterfly begins life as a tiny egg. The egg hatches into a caterpillar. The caterpillar eats and eats and eats until the time is ready. Then it spins a cocoon and sleeps. While the caterpillar sleeps, its body changes into a new creature. It changes into a butterfly. When we see butterflies, we can remember our Bible verse, "See, everything has become new!" (2 Corinthians 5:17), and we can remember Jesus.

Enjoy making and eating a butterfly sandwich with your child. Make your favorite sandwich and cut it into triangles. Make the butterfly's body by placing a pickle wedge in the center of a plate. Make the butterfly's wings by placing a sandwich triangle on each side of the pickle.

 **Jesus gives new life.**

PRESCHOOL 7   Permission granted to photocopy for local church use. © 1999 Abingdon Press.

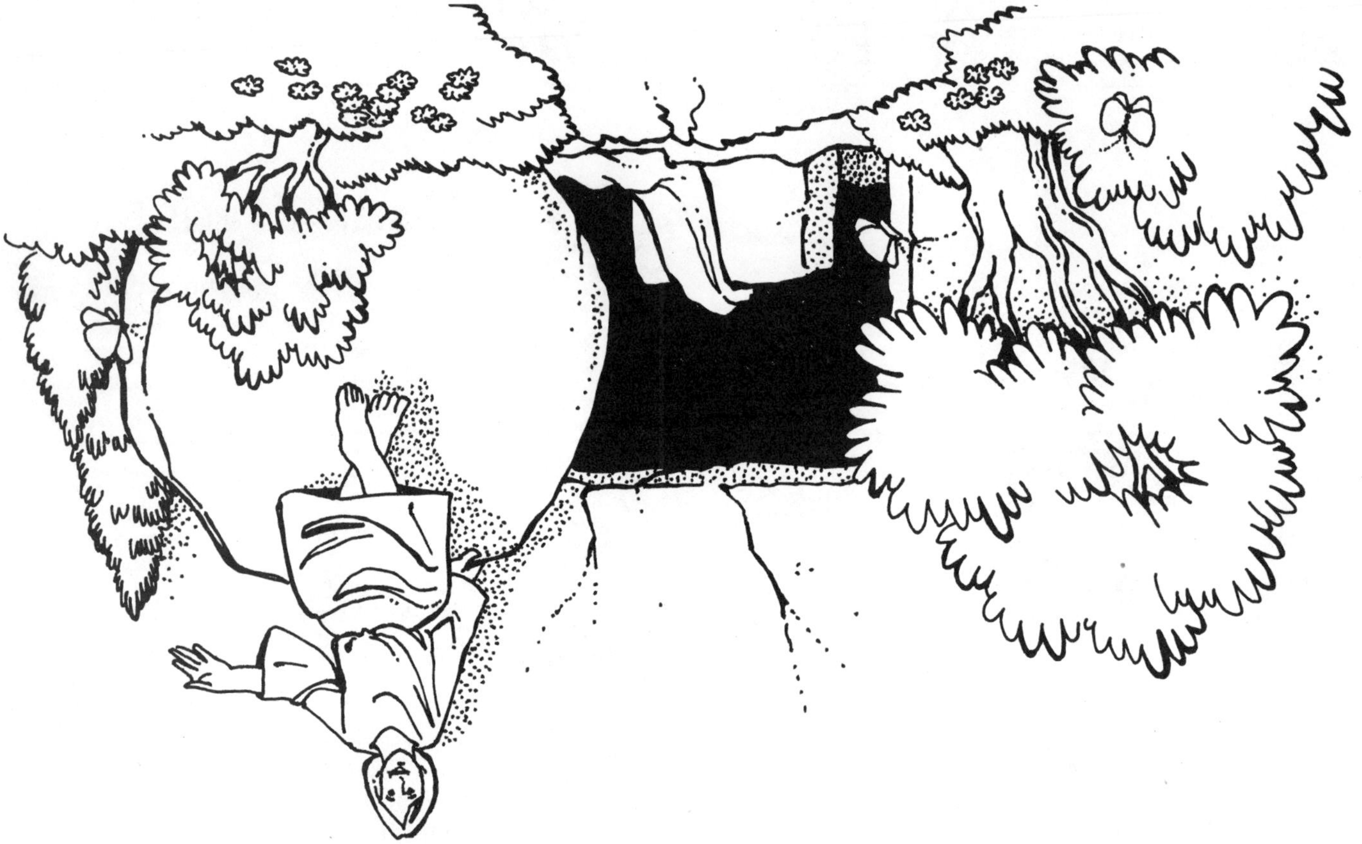

Reproducible 4A

Permission granted to photocopy for local church use. © 1999 Abingdon Press.

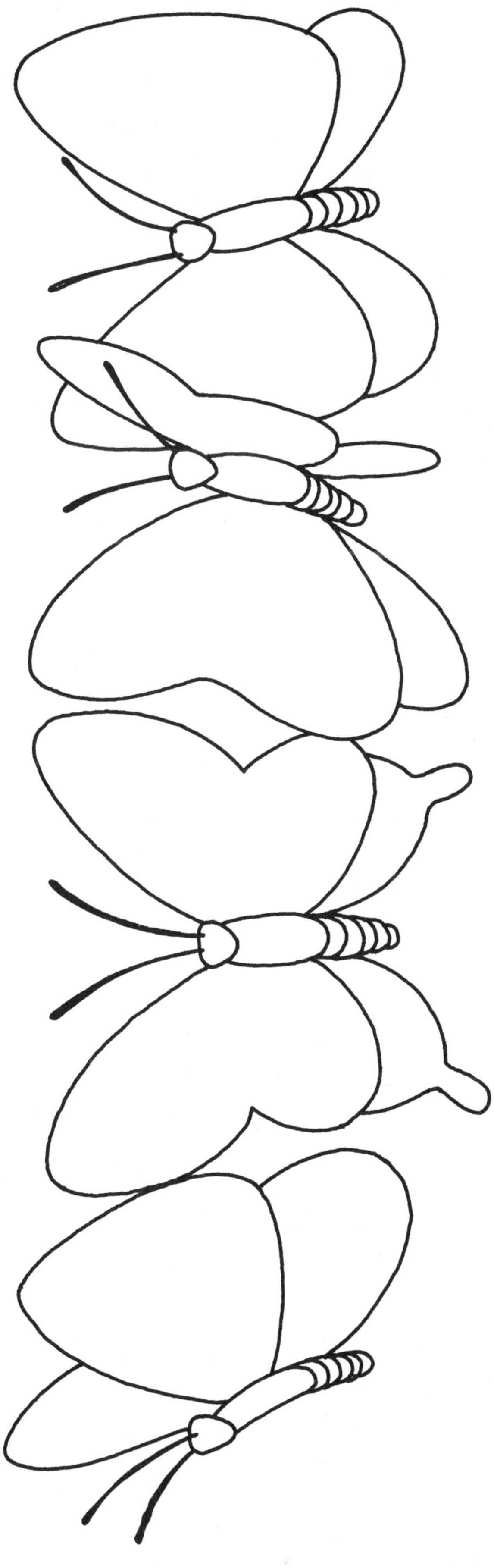

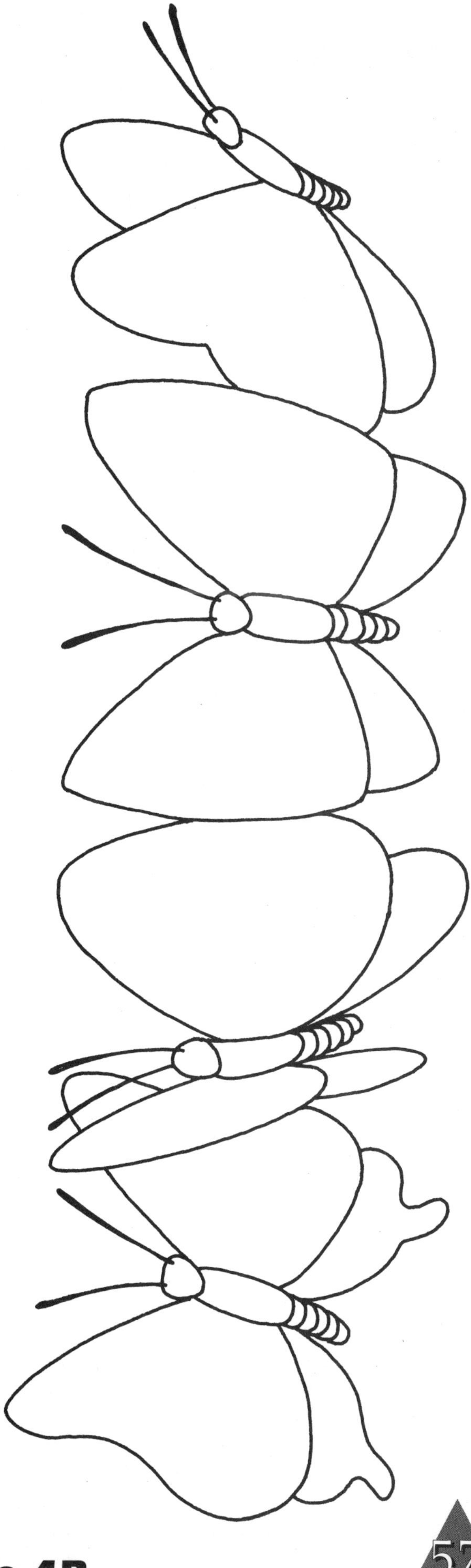

Reproducible 4B

Permission granted to photocopy for local church use. © 1999 Abingdon Press.

5 Bible Zone

Do You Believe?

Enter the Zone

Bible Verse
Stop your doubting, and believe!
John 20:27, *Good News Bible*

Bible Story
John 20:24–29

The women were the first to know of Jesus' resurrection. When they announced that not only was Jesus gone from the tomb, but also that they had seen him and touched him, the apostles thought it was just an idle tale. But this was just the first of the many appearances and visions that the whole company experienced.

On the evening of that first day of the week, the disciples were gathered together behind locked doors. Due to the events of the past few days, they were terrified that what had happened to their teacher and friend could just as easily happen to them. Suddenly Jesus appeared in their midst. Even though he was transformed from his resurrection, he was still as solid as a mortal. Those who experienced this visitation were filled with wonder and were eager to share the event with those who had not been there.

But there was one who, no matter how many times the others told him about Jesus' appearance, would not believe until he had actually seen and touched Jesus for himself. One week later when the disciples had gathered together, Jesus again came to them. This time Thomas was present. Jesus had Thomas touch the wounds that he had received upon the cross. Only then would Thomas believe that it was truly Jesus.

How often do we use the expression "seeing is believing" when referring to a seemingly impossible event? We rely on our senses to validate what we perceive to be true. Children relate to the world in a concrete fashion. So how do you teach someone about God? God cannot be seen or felt or touched or tasted or heard. And what about Jesus? We only have the stories that someone else wrote about him to inform us of who he was and what he did. The rest of the story must be accepted by the children on the basis of faith.

Sharing your faith helps the children understand that some things cannot be perceived in concrete terms. It also helps them to understand how others can accept these things and believe.

We believe in Jesus.

Scope the Zone

ZONE	TIME	SUPPLIES	ZILLIES®
Zoom Into the Zone			
Fan Fandango	10 minutes	Reproducible 5B, scissors, glue, small paper plates, crayons or markers	green crepe paper
Seeing Is Believing	10 minutes	Reproducibles 5A and 5B, scissors, bag	none
BibleZone®			
Praise Parade	5 minutes	fans (see page 60)	none
Do You Believe?	10 minutes	none	none
Bible Verse Buzz	5 minutes	Bible, BZ Bee	none
Sing!	5 minutes	cassette player, fans (see page 60)	Cassette
LifeZone			
Tell Thomas	10 minutes	none	none
Stop and Go	10 minutes	none	none
Bible Verse Songfest	5 minutes	none	none
Puppet Prayers	5 minutes	none	lamb puppet

Zillies® are found in the **BibleZone® FUNspirational® Kit.**

Zoom Into the Zone

Choose one or more activities to catch your children's interest.

Supplies:
Reproducible 5B, scissors, glue, small paper plates, crayons or markers

Zillies®:
green crepe paper

Fan Fandango

Photocopy and cut out two squares of the picture of Jesus (**Reproducible 5B**) for each child. You will use all the pictures in the "Seeing Is Believing" activity. Give each child two small paper plates and two pictures of Jesus. Let the children glue the pictures of Jesus onto their paper plates.

Say: Jesus died and was buried in a tomb. Two of Jesus' friends went to the tomb, but Jesus was not in the tomb. Jesus was alive! The friends were surprised and happy. They ran to tell the other friends that Jesus was alive! Let's make fans to wave and celebrate because Jesus is alive.

Encourage the children to decorate both of their paper plate fans by coloring them with crayons or markers. Help the children glue strips of **green crepe paper** to the edges of their fans.

Show the children how to hold a paper plate in each hand and wave the plates up and down. Set the fans aside to use with the "Praise Parade," page 61.

Supplies:
Reproducibles 5A and 5B, scissors, bag

Zillies®:
none

Seeing Is Believing

Photocopy and cut apart the picture cards (**Reproducibles 5A and 5B**). Make enough copies so there is at least one card for each child. Fold the cards on the dotted lines so that the pictures are inside. Place the pictures inside a bag. Have a child take a picture out of the bag without opening it and give it to you. Look at the picture without showing it to the children.

Say: I am holding a picture of a *(name of item pictured)*. **Do you believe me?** *(Have the children respond by saying yes or no. Then let the children see the picture.)* **Was what I told you true?** *(Let the children respond.)*

When you come to the blank card, make up an item *(horse, frog, fire engine)*. Continue the game until you have used all the pictures.

Say: Did you believe what I told you when you could not see the picture? Did you believe what I told you when you could see the picture? Today our Bible story is about one of Jesus' friends named Thomas. Thomas did not believe when he was told that Jesus was alive. After Thomas saw Jesus, he stopped doubting, and he believed.

BibleZone®

Bible Zone

Choose one or more activities to immerse your children in the Bible story.

Praise Parade

Use the following parade to lead your children around the room. Have the children hold their fans as they follow you. Repeat the verses as necessary to lead the children to your story area.

Here comes the praise parade.
(March around the room.)
Here comes the praise parade.
Follow me and march, march, march.
Here comes the praise parade.

Praise God, praise God,
(Stop marching; hold arms above head and shake hands.)
Let's praise God for Jesus.
(Clap hands.)
Praise God, praise God,
(Hold arms above head and shake hands.)
Let's praise God today.
(Clap hands.)
Hurray!
(Hold arms up above head and jump.)

Here comes the praise parade.
(Stomp around the room.)
Here comes the praise parade.
Follow me and stomp, stomp, stomp.
Here comes the praise parade.

Praise God, praise God,
(Stop stomping; hold arms above head and shake hands.)
Let's praise God for Jesus.
(Clap hands.)
Praise God, praise God,
(Hold arms above head and shake hands.)
Let's praise God today.
(Clap hands.)
Hurray!
(Hold arms up above head and jump.)

Supplies:
fans (see page 60)

Zillies®:
none

Bible Zone Story

Do You Believe?

by Sharilyn S. Adair

ave the children sit down in your story area.

Say: Today's story is about what happened to some friends of Jesus. Whenever you hear the words No, no! *in the story, I want you to cover your eyes with your hands so that you cannot see. Whenever you hear the words* Yes, yes!*, I want you to uncover your eyes.*

Before you begin the story, let the children practice covering and uncovering their eyes as you repeat, "No, no!" and "Yes, yes!" several times.

When Jesus died, his friends were not happy. **No, no!** *(Have the children cover their eyes with their hands.)* They were not happy at all. They were sad because they thought that they would never see their friend again. They gathered in a house where they could all be sad together.

But guess what happened? Jesus came right into that house where they were meeting. **Yes, yes!** *(Have the children uncover their eyes.)* Their friend Jesus was alive, and he was right there with them. Everybody could see him. Now they were excited and happy! Jesus visited with them for a while, and then he went away.

One friend, named Thomas, was not with the others when Jesus came to visit. The friends could hardly wait to see Thomas so that they could tell him what had happened.

"Thomas! Thomas!" they all shouted together, "Jesus is alive!"

"No, no!" *(Cover eyes.)* said Thomas. "You are wrong. Our friend Jesus died. He is not alive."

"Yes, Yes!" *(Uncover eyes.)* said the friends. "He is too alive. We saw him. Don't you believe us?"

"No, no!" *(Cover eyes.)* said Thomas. "I do not believe that Jesus is alive. I would have to see him to believe that. **Yes, yes!** *(Uncover eyes.)* I will only believe that Jesus is alive if I see him for myself."

A week went by. Then Thomas and the other friends gathered in the house again. The other friends were happy, but not Thomas. **No, no!** *(Cover eyes.)* He still did not believe that Jesus was alive.

Just then Jesus came into the room where Thomas and the other friends were meeting. "Thomas," said Jesus. "Stop your doubting and believe! You must have faith. Now do you see that I am alive?"

"Yes, yes!" *(Uncover eyes.)* said Thomas. "You are my Lord and my God. I know that you are alive."

"I am glad that you believe," said Jesus. "But you don't have to see me to believe that I am alive. It is even better to believe without seeing."

Now all of the friends of Jesus were happy, even Thomas.

Zone In With BZ Bee

Bible Verse Buzz

hoose a child to hold the Bible open to John 20:27.

Say: **Jesus died and was buried in a tomb. Two of Jesus' friends went to the tomb, but Jesus was not in the tomb. Jesus was alive! Today our Bible story is about one of Jesus' friends named Thomas. Thomas did not believe when he was told that Jesus was alive. After Thomas saw Jesus, he stopped doubting, and he believed.**

Say the Bible verse, "Stop your doubting, and believe!" (John 20:27, *Good News Bible*), for the children. Have the children say the Bible verse after you.

Turn your back to the children or hide your hands underneath a table or behind the **BibleZone® FUNspirational® Kit** lid as you place the **BZ Bee puppet** (see page 174) on your hand. Turn around or bring the puppet out where the children can see it.

Pretend to make the puppet talk. Change your voice for the puppet:

Bzzz. Bzzz. Bzzz. Hi, everybody! I'm BZ Bee. *Bzzz. Bzzz. Bzzz.* I like to taste fingers. Do you have fingers? Yum, yum, yum. Let me taste.

Go to each child. Encourage, but do not force, each child to hold up his or her fingers. Have BZ pretend to taste each child's fingers. Have BZ say things like:

Mmmm. Mmmm. You taste like honey.
Bzzz. Bzzz. You taste like strawberries.
Yumm. Yumm. You taste like blueberries.

After BZ has tasted each child's fingers, say:

Bzzz. Bzzz. Bzzz. I like to taste your fingers. They're yummy. (*Rub BZ's stomach.*)

Bzzz. Bzzz. Bzzz. I like something else even more than fingers.

I like the Bible. *Bzzz. Bzzz. Bzzz.* You heard a Bible story today. Who did not believe that Jesus was alive? *(Thomas)* Did Thomas believe when he saw Jesus? *(yes)*

Bzzz. Bzzz. Bzzz. After Thomas saw Jesus, he stopped doubting, and he believed.

 **We believe in Jesus.**

Bzzz. Bzzz. Bzzz. Let's say the Bible verse together.

"Stop your doubting, and believe!" (John 20:27, *Good News Bible*).

Have the children repeat the Bible verse with BZ Bee. Have BZ Bee say good-bye to the children. Put the puppet away.

Bible

Choose one or more activities to immerse your children in the Bible story.

Supplies:
cassette player, fans (see page 60)

Zillies®:
Cassette

Sing!

ave the children bring their fans (see page 60) and move to an open area of the room.

Say: Jesus died and was buried in a tomb. Two of Jesus' friends went to the tomb, but Jesus was not in the tomb. Jesus was alive! The friends ran to tell Jesus' friends the news. Jesus was alive! Let's wave our fans and celebrate because Jesus is alive.

Sing the song "For He's a Wonderful Savior" from the **Cassette.** The tune is "For He's a Jolly Good Fellow." Explain to the children that "Savior" is another name we call Jesus.

For He's a Wonderful Savior

For He's a wonderful Savior,
For He's a wonderful Savior,
For He's a wonderful Savior
And ev'ryone ought to know.
And ev'ryone ought to know.
Yes, ev'ryone ought to know.

For He's a wonderful Savior,
For He's a wonderful Savior,
For He's a wonderful Savior
And ev'ryone ought to know.

For He's the God of creation,
For He's the God of creation,
For He's the God of creation,
And ev'ryone ought to know.
And ev'ryone ought to know.
Yes, ev'ryone ought to know.

For He's the God of creation,
For He's the God of creation,
For He's the God of creation,
And ev'ryone ought to know.

So tell your friends about Jesus.
So tell your friends about Jesus.
So tell your friends about Jesus.
For ev'ryone ought to know.
And ev'ryone ought to know.
Yes, ev'ryone ought to know.

So tell your friends about Jesus.
So tell your friends about Jesus.
So tell your friends about Jesus.
For ev'ryone ought to know.

Writer: Ruth Schram
© 1995 New Spring Publishing/ASCAP
All Rights Reserved.
Used by permission of Brentwood-Benson Music Publishing, Inc.

From the Brentwood Music, Inc. recording *Mother Goose Gospel, vol. 2.*

Choose one or more activities to bring the Bible to life.

Tell Thomas

ave the children stand in a circle. Choose one child to be Thomas. Have Thomas stand in the middle of the circle.

Say: Jesus died and was buried in a tomb. Two of Jesus' friends went to the tomb, but Jesus was not in the tomb. Jesus was alive! The friends were surprised and happy. They ran to tell the other friends that Jesus was alive! Let's pretend that we are Jesus' friends. We will tell Thomas that Jesus is alive.

Have Thomas close his or her eyes. Choose a child from the circle. Have that child tiptoe behind Thomas, tap him or her on the shoulder, and say, "Jesus is alive!" Then have the child tiptoe back to the circle. Tell Thomas to open his or her eyes and guess who said, "Jesus is alive!" Give Thomas clues if she or he has trouble guessing. Continue the game with another child pretending to be Thomas.

At the end of the game say: Thomas did not believe when he was told that Jesus was alive. After Thomas saw Jesus, he stopped doubting, and he believed. We cannot see Jesus like Thomas did, but we can believe in Jesus.

 **We believe in Jesus.**

Supplies:
none

Zillies®:
none

Stop and Go

ave the children move to one side of the room.

Say: Thomas did not believe when he was told that Jesus was alive. When Thomas saw Jesus, Jesus told him to "Stop your doubting, and believe." That's our Bible verse for today, "Stop your doubting and believe!" (John 20:27, *Good News Bible*). *(Have the children repeat the verse.)* **When I say, "Go!" start tiptoeing across the room. When I say, "Stop!" stop moving and say the Bible verse.**

Say, "Go!" and have the children tiptoe across the room. Say, "Stop!" and have the children stop moving. Then have the children say the Bible verse, "Stop your doubting, and believe!" (John 20:27, *Good News Bible*).

Supplies:
none

Zillies®:
none

PRESCHOOL 7

Life Zone

Choose one or more activities to bring the Bible to life.

Supplies:
none

Zillies®:
none

Bible Verse Songfest

Say: Thomas did not believe when he was told that Jesus was alive. When Thomas saw Jesus, Jesus told him to "Stop your doubting and believe" (John 20:27, *Good News Bible*).

Sing the Bible verse with the children to the tune of "The Farmer in the Dell."

"Stop doubting and believe."
"Stop doubting and believe."
We know Jesus is alive.
"Stop doubting and believe."

Supplies:
none

Zillies®:
lamb puppet

Puppet Prayers

Have the children sit down. Show the children the **lamb puppet**.

Say: This is my puppet, Lambkins. What kind of animal is Lambkins? *(lamb, sheep)* **Lambs help us remember the new life God plans for us in God's world. Lambs also can help us remember that Jesus taught us about new life. Lambkins wants to help us praise God for Jesus and for new life.**

Hold up the lamb puppet and sing the following song to the tune of "Are You Sleeping?" Pretend that the puppet is singing one line, and have the children sing the repeating line after the puppet.

Here is Lambkins,
Here is Lambkins,
Come to say,
Come to say,
"Let's praise God for Jesus
"Let's praise God for Jesus
As we pray."
As we pray."

Pray: Thank you, God, for Jesus. Thank you, God, for new life. Amen.

Photocopy the **HomeZone®** newsletter to send home to parents.

Home Zone For Parents

Bible Verse
Stop your doubting, and believe!
John 20:27, Good News Bible

Bible Story
John 20:24–29

Do You Believe?

Today your child heard the story of Thomas, one of Jesus' disciples. When the other disciples told Thomas that Jesus was alive, he would not believe them until he had actually seen and touched Jesus for himself. When Thomas did see Jesus, he stopped doubting, and he believed.

We cannot see and touch Jesus as Thomas did. We are those who "have not seen and yet have come to believe" (John 20:29). We accept Jesus as our friend and savior on the basis of faith. Sharing your own faith with your child will help your child accept and believe the miracle of Jesus.

Believer Biscuits

Cut an English muffin in half. Help your child spread peanut butter over the muffin. Let your child use raisins to add two eyes and a smile on top of the peanut butter.

Remind your child that Jesus' friends were surprised and happy when they found out that Jesus was alive.

We believe in Jesus.

Reproducible 5A

Permission granted to photocopy for local church use. © 1999 Abingdon Press.

Reproducible 5B

6 Bible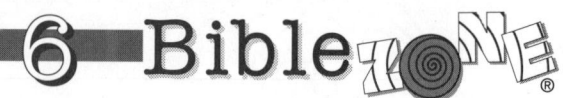

In the Beginning

Enter the Zone

Bible Verse
And God saw that it was good.
Genesis 1:25

Bible Story
Genesis 1:1–13

The Book of Genesis is a proclamation that God is the source of all Creation. It is a statement of faith that answers important questions for God's people. Although the Book of Genesis does not offer scientific explanations for how the world came to be, it does answer far more important questions about why God created and who we are in relationship to God. The Greek word *genesis* means "beginning." The Hebrews' stories told of God who was present at the beginning of the cosmos and upon whom all living things depended for their being. From these stories the people learned that nothing is independent, self-created, or self-sustaining. God is the source of all that exists.

The images in the Creation story describe Creation in the language of the Hebrews. For these early people the earth was the center of the universe. They thought the earth was flat, with a domed sky. In the sky there were windows to let the waters through.

Surely the Hebrew people would be amazed by the vast scientific knowledge we have of the universe today. But none of that scientific knowledge changes the wonder of God's creating. In fact, the more we learn about the universe, or the abilities of human beings, the more we marvel at the miracle of God's creation.

Young children learn with their senses. The stories of Creation offer many opportunities for the children to see, touch, feel, smell, or taste. Take advantages of these opportunities so that your children will experience Creation through their personal experiences.

Some children may ask, "Who made God?" According to the Bible, God simply was. God is. God always will be. This could be a difficult concept to communicate to children. Yet the children will have no trouble accepting God as the Creator of all that is. Because creation is a gift to all of us from God, caring for all that God created is not something we can choose to do; it is something God commands us to do.

God made our beautiful world.

Scope the Zone

ZONE	TIME	SUPPLIES	ZILLIES®
Zoom Into the Zone			
Tree Tales	15 minutes	Reproducible 6A, glue, crayons or markers	green crepe paper
True or False?	5 minutes	none	none
BibleZone®			
Walk This Way	5 minutes	none	none
Sign 'n Say	5 minutes	none	none
In the Beginning	10 minutes	none	fan, green crepe paper
Bible Verse Buzz	5 minutes	Bible, BZ Bee	none
Sing!	5 minutes	cassette player	Cassette
LifeZone			
Listen 'n Jump	10 minutes	Reproducible 6B, scissors	none
Creation Clay	5 minutes	none or ingredients for play dough (see page 168)	green and blue modeling clay
Nighttime Prayers	10 minutes	none	inflatable celestial ball

Zillies® are found in the **BibleZone® FUNspirational® Kit.**

PRESCHOOL 7

Zoom Into the Zone

Choose one or more activities to catch your children's interest.

Supplies:
Reproducible 6A, glue, crayons or markers

Zillies®:
green crepe paper

Tree Tales

Photocopy the tree trunk picture **(Reproducible 6A)** for each child. Give each child a picture. Let the children decorate the tree trunk with crayons or markers. Then give each child a short strip of **green crepe paper.** Let the children tear the crepe paper into small pieces. Have the children glue the pieces onto their trees to make leaves.

Say: God made our beautiful world. God made the sun and moon and stars. God made the plants and flowers and trees. God made the fish and the birds and the animals. God made you and me.

God made our beautiful world.

Have the children place their tree pictures on the floor in an open area of the room. Have the children stand beside their pictures.

Say: God made the sun that shines on the trees. *(Make a circle with arms over head.)* God made the rain that waters the trees. *(Wiggle fingers up and down for raindrops.)* God made the wind that blows the leaves on the trees. *(Move arms in large, sweeping movements.)* God made the birds that nest in the trees. *(Move arms up and down like wings.)* God made the squirrels that play in the trees. *(Skip around picture.)* God made the girls and boys that sit under the trees. *(Sit down beside picture.)*

Supplies:
none

Zillies®:
none

True or False?

Make the following statements about God's world. If the statement is true, have the children nod their heads yes and say, "Yes! God's world is good!" If the statement is false, have the children shake their heads no and say, "No! Not in God's world!"

God made clouds to float up in the sky.
Yes! God's world is good!
God made great big whales to swim in the sea.
Yes! God's world is good!
God made cats to bark, "Woof, woof!"
No! Not in God's world!
God made dogs to bark, "Woof, woof!"
Yes! God's world is good!

Choose one or more activities to immerse your children in the Bible story.

Walk This Way

Call the children by name either one at a time or in groups of two or three. Instruct the children to move to your story area with one of the following suggestions and sit down.

Pretend you are walking on clouds.
Pretend you are walking in mud.
Pretend you are walking on hot sand.
Pretend you are walking on rocks.

Supplies:
none

Zillies®:
none

Sign 'n Say

Say: **The Bible tells us God made our beautiful world. When God made the world, God saw that it was good.**

Teach the children the Bible verse, "And God saw that it was good" (Genesis 1:25), in American Sign Language.

Supplies:
none

Zillies®:
none

God — Point the index finger of your right hand, with the other fingers curled down. Bring the hand down and open the palm.

saw — Hold your fingers in a V-shape in front of your eyes. Move the hand forward.

good — Touch the fingers of your right hand to the lips. Move the hand forward and drop it into the open palm of the left hand.

Bible Zone Story

In the Beginning

by Sharilyn S. Adair

ave the children lie down in your story area. Have the **fan** ready to use. Tear **green crepe paper** into strips about thirty-six inches long. Have one on hand for each child.

Shh! shh! Lie down and close your eyes. Be very still. Let's pretend that we are lying like a big pool of water at the very beginning of the world. Everything is dark and quiet. We can't see anything or hear anything. Listen to how quiet it is. *(Pause.)*

At first we don't feel anything. But then God breathes a breath of fresh air on us. When you feel the air on your face, you may roll back and forth like waves on water. But don't move until you feel the air. And don't peek because the world is still dark, and we can't see anything. *(Fan each child's face in turn with the fan as you say, "Whoosh!")*

Now God has decided to make two different times: nighttime for sleeping when it is dark, and daytime for seeing things and running and playing. You may sit up. When I say, "Now it is day," open your eyes. When I say, "Now it is night," close your eyes. *(Repeat the two sentences three or four times. End with day.)*

God likes the night and day. Daytime is good for playing and for having fun. Nighttime is good for sleeping and for getting rest. God sees that night and day are good.

God wants the world to have a big blue sky over it. Stand up and reach high over your head. Pretend that your hands are the sky. *(Arch your arms above your head with the fingertips touching.)* The sky is very beautiful. God sees that the sky is good.

God has decided to make land in the water. Everyone lie down in our pool of water again. If I touch you, stand up and pretend to be land. *(Choose some children randomly.)* You might be a big tall mountain or a long flat beach full of sand. God likes the land and the water. Land is good for standing and running on. Water is good for wading and swimming in. God sees that land and water are good.

God wants the land to be beautiful. God makes plants and trees grow on the land. Everybody crouch like this *(Demonstrate.)*, and let's pretend to be growing plants. Let's stre-e-etch up and let our branches come out. *(Stand slowly and raise your arms up.)* Now we are plants. Let's let our leaves wave in the breeze. *(Give each child a crepe paper streamer. Let the children wave their streamers.)*

God likes the plants and trees. Plants can be food, and trees can give food and shade. God sees that plants and trees are good. God has made a beautiful world. Let's skip in a circle and wave our leaves. Let's say, "Hooray! Hooray for God's world!" *(Encourage the children to repeat the sentence with you several times. Let them skip and wave their streamers as long as they wish.)*

BibleZone®

In With BZ Bee

Bible Verse Buzz

hoose a child to hold the Bible open to Genesis 1:25.

Say: In the beginning, before there was anything, there was God. God made our beautiful world. God made the sun and moon and stars. God made the plants and flowers and trees. God made the fish and the birds and the animals. God made you and me. When God made the world, God saw that it was good.

Say the Bible verse, "And God saw that it was good" (Genesis 1:25), for the children. Have the children say the Bible verse after you.

Turn your back to the children or hide your hands underneath a table or behind the **BibleZone® FUNspirational® Kit** lid as you place the **BZ Bee puppet** (see page 174) on your hand. Turn around or bring the puppet out where the children can see it.

Pretend to make the puppet talk. Change your voice for the puppet:

Bzzz. Bzzz. Bzzz. Hi, everybody! I'm BZ Bee. *Bzzz. Bzzz. Bzzz.* I like to taste fingers. Do you have fingers? Yum, yum, yum. Let me taste.

Go to each child. Encourage, but do not force, each child to hold up his or her fingers. Have BZ pretend to taste each child's fingers. Have BZ say things like:

Mmmm. Mmmm. You taste like honey.
Bzzz. Bzzz. You taste like strawberries.
Yumm. Yumm. You taste like blueberries.

After BZ has tasted each child's fingers, say:

Bzzz. Bzzz. Bzzz. I like to taste your fingers. They're yummy. *(Rub BZ's stomach.)*

Bzzz. Bzzz. Bzzz. I like something else even more than fingers.

I like the Bible. *Bzzz. Bzzz. Bzzz.* You heard a Bible story today. Who made the world? *(God)*

Bzzz. Bzzz. Bzzz. The Bible tells us God made our beautiful world. When God made the world, God saw that it was good.

 **God made our beautiful world.**

Bzzz. Bzzz. Bzzz. Let's say the Bible verse together.

"And God saw that it was good" (Genesis 1:25).

Have the children repeat the Bible verse with BZ Bee. Have BZ Bee say good-bye to the children. Put the puppet away.

Choose one or more activities to immerse your children in the Bible story.

Supplies:
cassette player

Zillies®:
Cassette

Sing!

 ay: The Bible tells us God made our beautiful world. When God made the world, God saw that it was good.

Sing the song "He's Got the Whole World In His Hands" from the **Cassette**. Do the suggested motions as you sing the song with your children.

He's Got the Whole World In His Hands

He's got the whole world in His hands,
(Make a circle with arms in front of body.)
He's got the whole world in His hands,
He's got the whole world in His hands,
He's got the whole world in His hands.

He's got the wind and the rain in His hands,
(Sweep arms up; wiggle fingers and bring arms down.)
He's got the wind and the rain in His hands,
He's got the wind and the rain in His hands,
He's got the whole world in His hands.

He's got the tiny little baby in His hands.
(Pretend to rock baby.)
He's got the tiny little baby in His hands.
He's got the tiny little baby in His hands.
He's got the whole world in His hands.

He's got you and me and brother in His hands,
(Point to others; point to self.)
He's got you and me and sister in His hands,
He's got you and me and brother in His hands,
He's got the whole world in His hands.

He's got the whole world in His hands.
(Make a circle with arms in front of body.)
He's got the whole world in His hands.

© 1986 New Spring Publishing/ASCAP
All Rights Reserved.
Used by permission of Brentwood-Benson Music Publishing, Inc.

From the Brentwood Music, Inc. recording *Kids Sing Praise, vol. 1*.

Choose one or more activities to bring the Bible to life.

Listen 'n Jump

Photocopy and cut apart the creation pictures **(Reproducible 6B).** You will need as many cards as you have children. Have the children sit on the floor in a circle. Give each child a picture. Make sure each child can name what picture she or he is holding (*sun, clouds, mountains, water, flower, and tree*).

Say: God made our beautiful world. Listen carefully. I will name some of the things God made in our world. If you are holding the picture of the thing I name, jump up and shout, "Yeah, God!"

Read the following script and encourage the children to jump up and shout when they hear you name the pictures they are holding.

> God made our beautiful world. God made the **sun** to shine in the day. The **sun** warms the earth and helps the **flowers** and **trees** to grow. God made the **clouds** that float in the sky. Sometimes the **clouds** hide the **sun.** Sometimes the **clouds** become dark, and it begins to rain. The rain falls on the **flowers** and **trees** and helps them grow. God made the land with grass and sand and **mountains**. God made the salty **water** in the seas. God made the fresh **water** for animals and people to drink. God made the **water** in the streams that flow down the **mountains**. God made the **flowers** and **trees** that grow on the **mountains**. God made our beautiful world. And God saw that it was good!

Supplies:
Reproducible 6B, scissors

Zillies®:
none

Creation Clay

Give each child a small portion of **green clay** and a small portion of **blue clay**. If you have a large number of children, make play dough using the recipe printed on page 168. Encourage the children to roll the two colors together into a ball.

Say: Our blue and green clay balls remind me of how the earth looks from space. God made our beautiful world and saw that it was good.

Have the children hold their clay worlds in their hands. Have the children say the Bible verse, "And God saw that it was good" (Genesis 1:25).

Save the clay to use in other lessons.

Supplies:
none or ingredients for play dough (see page 168)

Zillies®:
green and blue modeling clay

Life

Choose one or more activities to bring the Bible to life.

Supplies:
none

Zillies®:
inflatable celestial ball

Nighttime Prayers

ave the children sit in a circle on the floor. Show the children the **inflatable celestial ball.**

Say: God made our beautiful world. God made the day, and God made the night. God made the sun to shine in the sky during the day. What do we see in the sky at night? *(moon and stars)* **God made the moon and stars that shine at night.** *(Turn off room lights, if possible; whisper.)* **Let's pretend it is nighttime. Let's look up into the sky at the moon and stars.**

Hold the ball up over your head. Sing the song printed below to the tune of "Do You Know the Muffin Man?" Let the children, holding the ball up high, pass the ball around the circle as you sing the song together.

> Do you know God made the moon,
> Made the moon, made the moon?
> Do you know God made the moon,
> And saw that it was good?
>
> Yes, we know God made the moon,
> Made the moon, made the moon.
> Yes, we know God made the moon,
> And saw that it was good.
>
> Do you know God made the stars,
> Made the stars, made the stars?
> Do you know God made the stars,
> And saw that it was good?
>
> Yes, we know God made the stars,
> Made the stars, made the stars.
> Yes, we know God made the stars,
> And saw that it was good.

Pray: Thank you, God, for the moon and stars that shine at night. Thank you, God, for our beautiful world. And thank you, God, for (*name each child*). **Amen.**

Photocopy the **HomeZone®** newsletter to send home to parents.

Home Zone For Parents

Bible Verse
And God saw that it was good. Genesis 1:25

Bible Story
Genesis 1:1–13

In the Beginning

Today your child heard part of the Creation story from the first chapter of Genesis. The Greek word *genesis* means "beginning." In the beginning, before there was anything, there was God.

Your child may ask, "Who made God?" According to the Bible, God simply was. God is. God always will be. This will be a difficult concept to communicate to children. Yet children have no trouble accepting God as the Creator of all that is. Use today's lesson as an opportunity to introduce your preschooler to God as Creator. Let your child hear you thank God for all God has created—including your child.

Sign 'n Say

Say the Bible verse, "And God saw that it was good" (Genesis 1:25), in American Sign Language.

God — Point the index finger of your right hand, with the other fingers curled down. Bring the hand down and open the palm.

saw — Hold your fingers in a V-shape in front of your eyes. Move the hand forward.

good — Touch the fingers of your right hand to the lips. Move the hand forward and drop it into the open palm of the left hand.

God made our beautiful world.

PRESCHOOL 7 Permission granted to photocopy for local church use. © 1999 Abingdon Press.

Reproducible 6A

Permission granted to photocopy for local church use. © 1999 Abingdon Press.

BIBLEZONE®

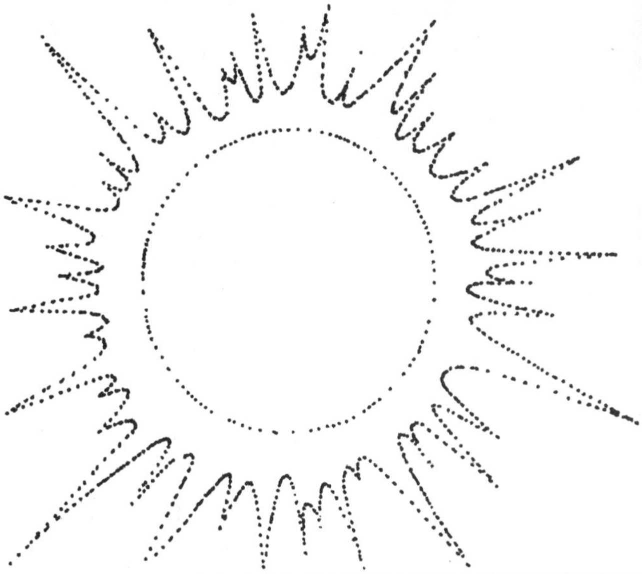

PRESCHOOL 7

Reproducible 6B

81

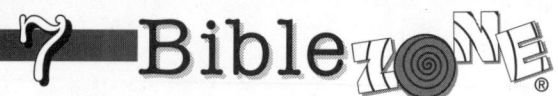

Sun, Moon, Stars

Enter the Zone

Bible Verse
And God saw that it was good.
Genesis 1:25

Bible Story
Genesis 1:14–19

When God spoke, there was Creation. God separated light from darkness, and there was day and night. God separated the waters, and there was sky and earth. God brought forth dry land from the seas. Finally, God set in place the sun, the moon, the stars, and the galaxies of the universe.

The poetic account of Creation in the Bible shows that the ancient Hebrews had little knowledge of the true nature of the universe as we know it today. To them the earth was the center of the universe. While they might have been aware of the phases of the moon, those people knew nothing of the planets that orbit the sun. They did not know that the sun was just another medium-sized star in a galaxy of many stars. How overwhelmed they would have been to hear about the billions upon billions of galaxies that exist beyond our own. Even scientists today are awed by the vastness.

But people then, as do people now, recognized the orderliness of creation. God had a plan for it all. God is the center of this finely tuned world. God provided everything necessary for life and for the organization of life. God is the Creator.

Young children like order and routines. Routines can help young children feel more secure and more confident. Help your young children understand God's plan for day and night through familiar routines that young children associate with day and night.

If your children express fear of the dark, help them understand that nighttime is part of God's plan for creation. Remind the children that God is always with us. God is with us during the day, and God is with us all through the night.

We thank God for the sun, moon, and stars.

Scope the Zone

ZONE	TIME	SUPPLIES	ZILLIES®
Zoom Into the Zone			
Starry Skies	10 minutes	Reproducible 7A	luminous chalk
Lights Turnover	10 minutes	none	none
BibleZone®			
Walk This Way	5 minutes	none	none
Sign 'n Say	5 minutes	none	none
Sun, Moon, Stars	10 minutes	Reproducible 7B	flashlight
Bible Verse Buzz	5 minutes	Bible, BZ Bee	none
Sing!	5 minutes	cassette player	Cassette
LifeZone			
Light Lessons	5 minutes	optional: blankets	flashlight
Sun Tag	10 minutes	none	none
Nighttime Prayers	10 minutes	none	inflatable celestial ball

◎ Zillies® are found in the **BibleZone® FUNspirational® Kit.**

PRESCHOOL 7

Zoom Into the Zone

Choose one or more activities to catch your children's interest.

Supplies:
Reproducible 7A

Zillies®:
luminous chalk

Starry Skies

Photocopy the Bible verse page **(Reproducible 7A)** for each child. Show the children the **luminous chalk** in the shape of sun, moon, and stars.

Say: God made our beautiful world. God made the sun, moon, and stars. The sun shines in the sky during the day. The moon and stars light up the night.

> **Zone IN: We thank God for the sun, moon, and stars.**

Let the children decorate their paper with the glow-in-the dark chalk. If possible, turn off the lights and darken the room. The chalk markings will glow. Display the starry chalk pictures in your story area.

Say: The Bible tells us that when God made the sun, moon, and stars, God saw that it was good.

Have the children repeat the Bible verse, "And God saw that it was good" (Genesis 1:25).

Supplies:
none

Zillies®:
none

Lights Turnover

Play a game with the children similar to "Fruit Basket Turnover." Have the children stand in a circle. Tell each child that he or she is either a sun, a moon, or a star. Have the child repeat what she or he is pretending to be.

Say: God made the sun, moon, and stars. God planned for the sun to shine during the day and the moon and the stars to shine during the night. Let's play a game. When I say, "God made the stars," everyone who is pretending to be a star change places in the circle. When I say, "God made the sun," everyone who is pretending to be a sun change places. When I say, "God made the moon," everyone who is pretending to be a moon change places. When I say, "Lights turnover," everyone change places.

Play the game with the children, then **say:** The Bible tells us that when God made the sun, moon, and stars, God saw that it was good.

Have the children repeat the Bible verse, "And God saw that it was good" (Genesis 1:25).

84

BibleZone®

Choose one or more activities to immerse your children in the Bible story.

Walk This Way

Call the children by name either one at a time or in groups of two or three. Instruct the children to move to your story area with one of the following suggestions and sit down.

Pretend you are walking in the hot sun.
Pretend you are walking at night when the moon is shining.
Pretend you are walking at night when it is so dark, it is hard to see.
Pretend you are a star moving through the night sky.

Supplies:
none

Zillies®:
none

Sign 'n Say

Say: The Bible tells us God made our beautiful world. When God made the world, God saw that it was good.

Teach the children the Bible verse, "And God saw that it was good" (Genesis 1:25), in American Sign Language.

God — Point the index finger of your right hand, with the other fingers curled down. Bring the hand down and open the palm.

saw — Hold your fingers in a V-shape in front of your eyes. Move the hand forward.

good — Touch the fingers of your right hand to the lips. Move the hand forward and drop it into the open palm of the left hand.

Supplies:
none

Zillies®:
none

Bible Zone Story

Sun, Moon, Stars

by Sharilyn S. Adair

Photocopy the sun, moon, and stars **(Reproducible 7B)**. Fold the page in half lengthwise so that the white half of the page is behind the black half. Have the **flashlight** on hand. Have the children sit down in your story area.

Say: When God was making our beautiful world, God filled the sky with different kinds of lights. Listen to my riddles, and see what I have lighted up. Can you guess each kind of light God made? At the end of each riddle, see if you can all say the name of the light together.

(Shine the flashlight behind the shape of the sun.)
I'm big and round and very bright.
I'm seen by day, but not by night.
When you're outside and having fun,
I shine on you,
For I'm the _____. *(sun)*

(Shine the flashlight behind the shape of the moon.)
I'm not as bright or far away.
I shine by night, but not by day.
Sometimes I'm round as a balloon;
Sometimes I'm skinny.
I'm the _____. *(moon)*

(Shine the flashlight behind the shape of the stars.)
We twinkle in the nighttime sky.
To see us you must look up high.
We are not planets, such as Mars.
We're little lights.
We are the _____. *(stars)*

God planned for stars and moon and sun
To shine their light for everyone.
When each was working as it should,
God saw that all these lights were good.

In With BZ Bee

Bible Verse Buzz

hoose a child to hold the Bible open to Genesis 1:25.

Say: God made our beautiful world. God made the sun, moon, and stars. The sun shines in the sky during the day. The moon and stars light up the night. The Bible tells us that when God made the sun, moon, and stars, God saw that it was good.

Say the Bible verse, "And God saw that it was good" (Genesis 1:25), for the children. Have the children say the Bible verse after you.

Turn your back to the children or hide your hands underneath a table or behind the **BibleZone® FUNspirational® Kit** lid as you place the **BZ Bee puppet** (see page 174) on your hand. Turn around or bring the puppet out where the children can see it.

Pretend to make the puppet talk. Change your voice for the puppet:

Bzzz. Bzzz. Bzzz. Hi, everybody! I'm BZ Bee. *Bzzz. Bzzz. Bzzz.* I like to taste fingers. Do you have fingers? Yum, yum, yum. Let me taste.

Go to each child. Encourage, but do not force, each child to hold up his or her fingers. Have BZ pretend to taste each child's fingers. Have BZ say things like:

Mmmm. Mmmm. You taste like honey.
Bzzz. Bzzz. You taste like strawberries.
Yumm. Yumm. You taste like blueberries.

After BZ has tasted each child's fingers, say:

Bzzz. Bzzz. Bzzz. I like to taste your fingers. They're yummy. *(Rub BZ's stomach.)*

Bzzz. Bzzz. Bzzz. I like something else even more than fingers.

I like the Bible. *Bzzz. Bzzz. Bzzz.* You heard a Bible story today. What did God make to light up the day? *(sun)* What did God make to light up the night? *(moon and stars)*

Bzzz. Bzzz. Bzzz. The Bible tells us God made the sun, moon, and stars. When God made the sun, moon, and stars, God saw that it was good.

 **We thank God for the sun, moon, and stars.**

Bzzz. Bzzz. Bzzz. Let's say the Bible verse together.

"And God saw that it was good" (Genesis 1:25).

Have the children repeat the Bible verse with BZ Bee. Have BZ Bee say good-bye to the children. Put the puppet away.

Bible

Choose one or more activities to immerse your children in the Bible story.

Supplies:
cassette player

Zillies®:
Cassette

Sing!

Say: **The Bible tells us God made our beautiful world. When God made the world, God saw that it was good. Let's sing a song to thank God for the world.**

Sing the song "Thank You, God" from the **Cassette.** The tune is "Three Blind Mice."

Thank You, God

Thank You, God,
Thank You, God,
For Your world,
For Your world.

I see You in the flowers and trees,
The humming bird and the honey bees,
It's such a beautiful world to me,
Oh, thank You, God,
Thank You, God.

Thank You, God,
Thank You, God,
For Your world,
For Your world.

I see You in the flowers and trees,
The humming bird and the honey bees,
It's such a beautiful world to me,
Oh, thank You, God,
Thank You, God.

Writer: Pam Andrews
© 1995 New Spring Publishing/ASCAP
All Rights Reserved.
Used by permission of Brentwood-Benson Music Publishing, Inc.

From the Brentwood-Benson Music, Inc. recording *Kid's Musical Yearbook.*

Choose one or more activities to bring the Bible to life.

Light Lessons

You will need to be in a room or space that can be darkened for this activity. If your room can be darkened, plan to do this activity in your story area. If your room cannot be darkened, take the children to a room that can (a room without windows). Or cover a work table with blankets. Lift the sides of the blanket so that it is light under the table.

Turn on all the lights in the room. Take the **flashlight** and sit on the floor or under the table with the children. Turn on the flashlight.

Ask: Can you see the light from the flashlight very well?

Turn off all the lights in the room. If you are sitting under the table, lower the blankets to make a dark space under the table.

Ask: What happens to the light from the flashlight when it gets dark? Does the light become easier to see? harder to see?

Say: God made the sun and moon and stars. When the sun is shining brightly, we cannot see the light from the moon and stars. When it is night, and the sun is not shining, we can see the light from the moon and stars. We thank God for the sun, moon, and stars.

Supplies:
optional: blankets

Zillies®:
flashlight

Sun Tag

Have the children move to an open area of the room.

Say: Let's pretend that you are stars and I am the sun. It is night, and all the stars are twinkling in the sky.

Have the children move about the room as stars.

Say: Now it's almost morning. Here comes the sun. When the sun is shining, no one can see the stars twinkling in the sky. If the sun tags you, crouch down and be very still.

Pretend to be the sun and tag each child. When a child is tagged, have her or him crouch down and be still.

When all the children have been tagged, **say: We thank God for the sun, moon, and stars.**

Supplies:
none

Zillies®:
none

Choose one or more activities to bring the Bible to life.

Supplies:
none

Zillies®:
inflatable celestial ball

Nighttime Prayers

ave the children sit in a circle on the floor. Show the children the **inflatable celestial ball.**

Say: God made our beautiful world. God made the day, and God made the night. God made the sun to shine in the sky during the day. What do we see in the sky at night? *(moon and stars)* **God made the moon and stars that shine at night.** *(Turn off room lights, if possible; whisper.)* **Let's pretend it is nighttime. Let's look up into the sky at the moon and stars.**

Hold the ball up over your head. Sing the song printed below to the tune of "Do You Know the Muffin Man?" Let the children, holding the ball up high, pass the ball around the circle as you sing the song together.

> Do you know God made the moon,
> Made the moon, made the moon?
> Do you know God made the moon,
> And saw that it was good?
>
> Yes, we know God made the moon,
> Made the moon, made the moon.
> Yes, we know God made the moon,
> And saw that it was good.
>
> Do you know God made the stars,
> Made the stars, made the stars?
> Do you know God made the stars,
> And saw that it was good?
>
> Yes, we know God made the stars,
> Made the stars, made the stars.
> Yes, we know God made the stars,
> And saw that it was good.

Pray: Thank you, God, for the moon and stars that shine at night. Thank you, God, for our beautiful world. And thank you, God, for *(name each child).* **Amen.**

Photocopy the **HomeZone®** newsletter to send home to parents.

Home Zone For Parents

Sun, Moon, Stars

Today's Bible story centers around the creation of the sun, moon, and stars. God separated light from darkness, and there was day and night. God separated the waters, and there was sky and earth. God brought forth dry land from the seas. Finally, God set in place the sun, the moon, the stars, and the galaxies of the universe.

Young children like order and routines. Routines can help young children feel more secure and more confident. Help your child understand God's plan for day and night through familiar routines that young children associate with day and night.

Bible Verse
And God saw that it was good.   Genesis 1:25

Bible Story
Genesis 1:14–19

Moon Balls

2 cups peanut butter
2 cups raisins
1⅓ cups honey
2 cups dry milk
3½ cups graham cracker crumbs

Mix 3 cups graham cracker crumbs with dry milk and raisins. Save ½ cup of graham cracker crumbs to use later. Mix in honey and peanut butter. Roll into small balls.

Place ½ cup of graham cracker crumbs into a large resealable plastic bag. Place three or four balls into the bag and seal shut. Shake the bag to cover the balls with graham cracker crumbs. Remove the balls and place them on a baking sheet or plate. Chill before eating.

We thank God for the sun, moon, and stars.

And God saw that it was good. Genesis 1:25

Reproducible 7A

PRESCHOOL 7

Reproducible 7B
Permission granted to photocopy for local church use.
© 1999 Abingdon Press.

8 Bible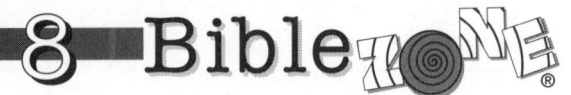

Fish and Birds

Enter the Zone

Bible Verse
And God saw that it was good.
Genesis 1:25

Bible Story
Genesis 1:20–23

Once the earth was ready, God continued to create by making living creatures of many kinds. There were fish and other creatures to swim in the sea. There were many kinds of animals to walk on the land. And there were birds to fly in the air above the ground. Today the focus of the lesson is the Biblical account of the creation of creatures that live in the sea and creatures that fly in the air.

With the creation of animals in the waters and in the air comes a blessing. While Creation has been affirmed as good, this is the first time a blessing is given.

The blessing is a meaningful image in the Old Testament. With a blessing one person gives power or vitality to another. In Creation this blessings shows that the animals of the water and air have an important relationship and value to God.

Preschool children are just beginning to classify information. They can understand that there are creatures that fly through the air and creatures that move in the water. There are creatures that live and move on the land. And there are people.

Introducing these different groups of creatures will help the children sort information about God's world. Use the activities in this lesson and in the lessons on animals and people to help the children experience what is special about each one of the groups.

Just as God blessed the animals that live in the water and the animals that fly in the air, God blesses you. Take a few moments and think about God's blessings in your life. Say a prayer of thanksgiving for those blessings.

We thank God for fish and birds.

Scope the Zone

ZONE	TIME	SUPPLIES	ZILLIES®
Zoom Into the Zone			
Fish or Bird?	10 minutes	Reproducible 8A, scissors	none
Sea or Sky?	10 minutes	Reproducible 8B, crayons or markers	fish stickers, bird stickers
BibleZone®			
Walk This Way	5 minutes	none	none
Sign 'n Say	5 minutes	none	none
Fish and Birds	10 minutes	none	none
Bible Verse Buzz	5 minutes	Bible, BZ Bee	none
Sing!	5 minutes	cassette player	Cassette
LifeZone			
Just Ducky	10 minutes	dishpan, water; or blue construction paper	plastic ducks, fish stickers, bird stickers
Fishy Fun	10 minutes	none	inflatable dolphin ring toss
Nighttime Prayers	10 minutes	none	inflatable celestial ball

Zillies® are found in the **BibleZone® FUNspirational® Kit**.

Zoom Into the Zone

Choose one or more activities to catch your children's interest.

Supplies:
Reproducible 8A, scissors

Zillies®:
none

Fish or Bird?

hotocopy and cut apart at least two sets of the fish and bird picture cards **(Reproducible 8A)**. Mix up the pictures and place them on the table or rug. Let the children enjoy matching the pictures.

Say: God made the fish and other animals that live in the water. God made the birds and other animals that fly.

> **We thank God for fish and birds.**

Have the children sort the pictures. Tell the children to put all the bird pictures together and all the fish pictures together.

Supplies:
Reproducible 8B, crayons or markers

Zillies®:
fish stickers, bird stickers

Sea or Sky?

hotocopy the sky and sea pictures **(Reproducible 8B)** for each child. Let the children decorate the pictures with crayons or markers.

Say: This is a picture of the sky. *(Point to the sky picture.)* **What animals did God make that fly in the sky?** *(birds, butterflies, bumblebees)* **This is a picture of the sea.** *(Point to the sea picture.)* **What animals did God make to live in water?** *(fish, seahorses, crabs)*

Give each child some of the **bird and fish stickers.** Let the children choose where to put the stickers on their pictures. Encourage, but do not force, the children to put the bird stickers in the sky and the fish stickers in the water.

Say: God made the birds that fly high in the sky. God made the fish that swim in the water.

> **We thank God for fish and birds.**

BIBLEZONE®

Choose one or more activities to immerse your children in the Bible story.

Walk This Way

Supplies: none

Zillies®: none

Call the children by name either one at a time or in groups of two or three. Instruct the children to move to your story area with one of the following suggestions and sit down.

Pretend you are a fish swimming in a river.
Pretend you are a bird flying in the sky.
Pretend you are a crab walking on the sand.
Pretend you are a bumblebee flying from flower to flower.

Sign 'n Say

Supplies: none

Zillies®: none

Say: **The Bible tells us God made our beautiful world. When God made the world, God saw that it was good.**

Teach the children the Bible verse, "And God saw that it was good" (Genesis 1:25), in American Sign Language.

God — Point the index finger of your right hand, with the other fingers curled down. Bring the hand down and open the palm.

saw — Hold your fingers in a V-shape in front of your eyes. Move the hand forward.

good — Touch the fingers of your right hand to the lips. Move the hand forward and drop it into the open palm of the left hand.

BibleZone Story

Fish and Birds

by Sharilyn S. Adair

Have the children stand in a circle in your story area. Explain to the children that they can help you tell today's story by pretending to swim like fish or to fly like birds whenever you do. Show them how to put their palms together in front of them and to weave their hands back and forth to be fish swimming. Have them hold their arms out to the sides at shoulder level and raise them up and down like flapping wings to be birds flying.

When God shaped the earth and planted the trees,
The sky still looked empty, and so did the seas.
God knew what to do; so God filled up the sky:
With all kinds of creatures that knew how to fly.

Let's all be birds. *(Lead the children around the table or around the room as you flap your arms during the next lines.)*

There were eagles and thrushes and whippoorwills too.
There were blackbirds and red birds and birds that were blue.
There were crows and canaries and big birds called fowls.
And for flying at night God created the owls—whoooo!

(Stop moving.)
And into the waters God placed with a swish
Some wonderful, beautiful creatures called fish.
In oceans and rivers and lakes among hills,
Fish breathed underwater by using their gills.

Let's all be fish. *(Lead the children around the table or around the room as you make the swimming motion for fish during the next lines.)*

There were porgies and flounders and codfish and trout.
There were rockfish and angelfish swimming about.
And then besides fish God created some whales
And tiny sea animals shaped just like snails.

(Stop moving.)
With skies filled with birds and seas filled with fishes,
All put in their places because of God's wishes,
God looked at this work as only God could
And blessing the creatures, God saw it was good.

Zone In With BZ Bee

Bible Verse Buzz

 Choose a child to hold the Bible open to Genesis 1:25.

Say: God made the fish and other animals that live in the water. God made the birds and other animals that fly. The Bible tells us that when God made the fish and the birds, God saw that it was good.

Say the Bible verse, "And God saw that it was good" (Genesis 1:25), for the children. Have the children say the Bible verse after you.

Turn your back to the children or hide your hands underneath a table or behind the **BibleZone® FUNspirational® Kit** lid as you place the **BZ Bee puppet** (see page 174) on your hand. Turn around or bring the puppet out where the children can see it.

Pretend to make the puppet talk. Change your voice for the puppet:

Bzzz. Bzzz. Bzzz. Hi, everybody! I'm BZ Bee. *Bzzz. Bzzz. Bzzz.* I like to taste fingers. Do you have fingers? Yum, yum, yum. Let me taste.

Go to each child. Encourage, but do not force, each child to hold up his or her fingers. Have BZ pretend to taste each child's fingers. Have BZ say things like:

Mmmm. Mmmm. You taste like honey.
Bzzz. Bzzz. You taste like strawberries.
Yumm. Yumm. You taste like blueberries.

After BZ has tasted each child's fingers, say:

Bzzz. Bzzz. Bzzz. I like to taste your fingers. They're yummy. *(Rub BZ's stomach.)*

Bzzz. Bzzz. Bzzz. I like something else even more than fingers.

I like the Bible. *Bzzz. Bzzz. Bzzz.* What animals did God make to live in the water? (*fish, seahorses, crabs*) What animals did God make to fly in the sky? (*birds, butterflies, bumblebees*)

Bzzz. Bzzz. Bzzz. The Bible tells us God made fish and birds. When God saw the fish and birds, God saw that it was good.

 **We thank God for fish and birds.**

Bzzz. Bzzz. Bzzz. Let's say the Bible verse together.

"And God saw that it was good" (Genesis 1:25).

Have the children repeat the Bible verse with BZ Bee. Have BZ Bee say good-bye to the children. Put the puppet away.

Bible

Choose one or more activities to immerse your children in the Bible story.

Supplies:
cassette player

Zillies®:
Cassette

Sing!

lay the song "If I Were a Butterfly" from the **Cassette.** Let the children pretend to be the animals named.

If I Were a Butterfly

If I were a butterfly
I'd thank You, Lord that I could fly;
And if I were a robin in a tree
I'd thank You, Lord, that I could sing.
And if I were a fish in the sea
I'd wiggle my tail and I'd giggle with glee.
But I just thank you Father for making me me.

'Cause You gave me a heart
And you gave me a smile,
You gave me Lord Jesus
And you made me Your child.
And I just thank you Father for making me me.

If I were an elephant
I'd thank You, Lord by raising my trunk,
And if I were a kangaroo
Oh I'd just hop right up to You.
And if I were an octopus
I'd thank You, Lord for my good looks.
But I just thank you Father for making me me.

'Cause You gave me a heart
And you gave me a smile,
You gave me Lord Jesus
And you made me Your child.
And I just thank you Father for making me me.

If I were a wiggley worm
I'd thank You, Lord that I could squirm;
And if I were a crocodile
I'd thank You, Lord that I could smile.
And if I were a fuzzy, wuzzy bear,
I'd thank You, Lord for my fuzzy, wuzzy hair.
But I just thank You, Father for making me me.

'Cause You gave me a heart
And you gave me a smile,
You gave me Lord Jesus
And you made me Your child.
And I just thank you Father for making me me.
And I just thank You, Father for making me me.

© 1995 New Spring Publishing/ASCAP
All Rights Reserved.
Used by permission of Brentwood-Benson Music Publishing, Inc.

From the Brentwood-Benson Music Publishing, Inc. recording *It's a Great Day to Praise the Lord.*

Life Zone

Choose one or more activities to bring the Bible to life.

Just Ducky

Place **fish stickers** on the bottoms of three of the **plastic ducks**. Place **bird stickers** on the bottoms of the remaining three plastic ducks. Partially fill a dishpan with water. Place the ducks in the water.

Have the children sit in a circle. Place the dishpan and the ducks in the center of the circle. If you choose not to float the ducks in water, set the ducks on a piece of blue construction paper.

Choose a child to pick a duck out of the water and look at the sticker on the bottom.

Ask: Do you see a bird or a fish? Does it swim in the water or fly in the air?

If the duck has a fish sticker on the bottom, have the child put the duck back in the water and pretend to swim around the outside of the circle back to her or his spot. If the duck has a bird sticker on the bottom, have the child put the duck back in the water and pretend to fly around the outside of the circle.

When all the children have had a turn choosing a duck and moving around the circle, **say: God made fish that swim in the water and birds that fly in the air.**

 **We thank God for fish and birds.**

Supplies:
dishpan, water; or blue construction paper

Zillies®:
plastic ducks, fish stickers, bird stickers

Fishy Fun

Inflate the **dolphin** and place it in an open area of the room. Have the children line up in front of the dolphin. Let the line begin fairly close to the dolphin.

Give the first child one of the rings. Let the child try to toss the ring over the dolphin's nose. After the toss (whether the child rings the nose or not) have all the children clap their hands and shout, "And God saw that it was good" (Genesis 1:25). Continue until every child has had a turn.

Supplies:
none

Zillies®:
inflatable dolphin ring toss

Life

Choose one or more activities to bring the Bible to life.

Supplies:
none

Zillies®:
inflatable celestial ball

Nighttime Prayers

Have the children sit in a circle on the floor. Show the children the **inflatable celestial ball.**

Say: God made our beautiful world. God made the day, and God made the night. God made the sun to shine in the sky during the day. What do we see in the sky at night? *(moon and stars)* **God made the moon and stars that shine at night.** *(Turn off room lights, if possible; whisper.)* **Let's pretend it is nighttime. Let's look up into the sky at the moon and stars.**

Hold the ball up over your head. Sing the song printed below to the tune of "Do You Know the Muffin Man?" Let the children, holding the ball up high, pass the ball around the circle as you sing the song together.

> Do you know God made the moon,
> Made the moon, made the moon?
> Do you know God made the moon,
> And saw that it was good?
>
> Yes, we know God made the moon,
> Made the moon, made the moon.
> Yes, we know God made the moon,
> And saw that it was good.
>
> Do you know God made the stars,
> Made the stars, made the stars?
> Do you know God made the stars,
> And saw that it was good?
>
> Yes, we know God made the stars,
> Made the stars, made the stars.
> Yes, we know God made the stars,
> And saw that it was good.

Pray: Thank you, God, for the moon and stars that shine at night. Thank you, God, for our beautiful world. And thank you, God, for *(name each child).* **Amen.**

Photocopy the **HomeZone®** newsletter to send home to parents.

Home Zone For Parents

Bible Verse
And God saw that it was good.   Genesis 1:25

Bible Story
Genesis 1:20–23

Fish and Birds

Once the earth was ready, God continued to create by making living creatures of many kinds. There were fish and other creatures to swim in the sea. There were many kinds of animals to walk on the land. And there were birds to fly in the air above the ground. Today the focus of the lesson is the Biblical account of the creation of creatures that live in the sea and creatures that fly in the air.

Preschool children are just beginning to classify information. They can understand that there are creatures that fly through the air and creatures that move in the water. There are creatures that live and move on the land. And there are people. Introducing these different groups of creatures will help your child sort information about God's world.

Fish Nibblers

2 tablespoons margarine or butter
2½ cups O-shaped cereal
1½ cups pretzel sticks
1 cup small fish-shaped crackers
2 teaspoons Worcestershire sauce

Melt butter or margarine. Mix the Worcestershire sauce into the melted butter. Place all the ingredients in a 2-quart resealable plastic bag. Securely seal the bag and shake it until the cereal, pretzels, and crackers are evenly coated with the sauce. Pour the mixture into a large microwave-safe bowl. Microwave on high for 3 to 3½ minutes. Stop and stir every minute. Spread on paper towels to cool.

Enjoy nibbling on this fishy snack with your child. Thank God for fish.

We thank God for fish and birds.

PRESCHOOL 7   Permission granted to photocopy for local church use. © 1999 Abingdon Press.

Reproducible 8A

9 Bible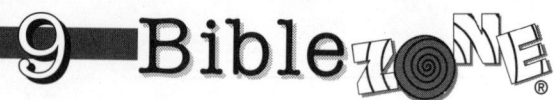

Animals

Enter the

Bible Verse
And God saw that it was good.
Genesis 1:25

Bible Story
Genesis 1:24-25

There was land and sea and sky. There were plants in abundance. There was warmth and light, and day and night. There were the seasons, as God prepared the earth for a more sophisticated form of life. God then made living creatures of many kinds. First God filled the waters with fish and other water-dwelling creatures. Then God filled the air above the earth with birds. Finally, God brought forth creatures of infinite diversity to walk upon the land.

God created animals to share the earth with the plants and, eventually, with human beings. There were animals to provide food, clothing, building materials, and transportation. There were animals that played their part in the balance of all of nature. And there were animals that would provide comfort and companionship for human beings.

Once again we discover that God planned for creation to continue. Animals were given God's blessing and the ability to reproduce more of their own kind. God's creation is truly a continuing process.

Children love animals. But do not assume that every child has had or will have an animal. Many children are not in a position to keep animals as pets. City children may not come into contact with animals, except cats or dogs. Some children may be allergic to animals.

But even with these limitations, we can talk about being responsible for the other creatures that share God's creation. We can help children understand that they share God's world with these creatures, and we can help them see the importance of being kind to all creatures. Animals have needs of their own, in addition to contributing to our lives. When a child learns to appreciate an animal, he or she learns to treat this animal with respect, and this may carry over to the child's treatment of other people.

We thank God for all the animals.

Scope the Zone

ZONE	TIME	SUPPLIES	ZILLIES®
Zoom Into the Zone			
Fishy Fun	10 minutes	none	inflatable dolphin ring toss
Where's the Mouse?	10 minutes	Reproducible 9A (top), scissors, tape	none
BibleZone®			
Walk This Way	5 minutes	none	none
Sign 'n Say	5 minutes	none	none
Animals	10 minutes	none	none
Bible Verse Buzz	5 minutes	Bible, BZ Bee	none
Sing!	5 minutes	cassette player	Cassette
LifeZone			
Turtle Races	15 minutes	Reproducibles 9B and 9A (bottom); scissors; crayons; newspapers; glue, tape, or stapler and staples	none
Four-Fingered Fun	5 minutes	none	zoo finger puppets
Nighttime Prayers	10 minutes	none	inflatable celestial ball

Zillies® are found in the **BibleZone® FUNspirational® Kit.**

Zoom Into the Zone

Choose one or more activities to catch your children's interest.

Supplies:
none

Zillies®:
inflatable dolphin
ring toss

Fishy Fun

Inflate the **dolphin** and place it in an open area of the room. Have the children line up in front of the dolphin. Let the line begin fairly close to the dolphin.

Give the first child one of the rings. Let the child try to toss the ring over the dolphin's nose. After the toss (whether the child rings the nose or not) have all the children clap their hands and shout, "And God saw that it was good" (Genesis 1:25). Continue until every child has had a turn.

Say: God made fish to swim in the water and birds to fly in the air. But God was not finished. God made many, many more animals. God made animals that crawled and hopped and slithered. God made animals with fur and animals with scales. God made all the animals.

We thank God for all the animals.

Supplies:
Reproducible 9A (top), scissors, tape

Zillies®:
none

Where's the Mouse?

Photocopy and cut out the mouse (**Reproducible 9A, top**). Tape the mouse together as pictured on the page. Have the children move to an open area of the room.

Say: God made all the animals. God made great big animals like elephants. (Have the children pretend to be elephants.) **God made smaller animals like cats.** (Have the children pretend to be cats.) **And God made tiny animals like mice.** (Have the children pretend to be mice.)

Have the children sit down on the floor. Show the children the paper mouse.

Say: Let's pretend that we are cats. While all the cats are sleeping, I will hide the mouse somewhere in the room. When I say, "Squeak! Squeak!", the cats can wake up and start looking for the mouse.

Have the children pretend to take a cat nap and to close their eyes while you hide the mouse somewhere in the room. Then let the cats look all around until someone finds the mouse. Play the game several times.

Choose one or more activities to immerse your children in the Bible story.

Walk This Way

Call the children by name either one at a time or in groups of two or three. Instruct the children to move to your story area with one of the following suggestions and sit down.

Pretend you are a monkey swinging from limb to limb.
Pretend you are a rabbit hopping through the forest.
Pretend you are a snake crawling through the desert.
Pretend you are a tiger walking through the jungle.

Supplies:
none

Zillies®:
none

Sign 'n Say

Say: The Bible tells us God made our beautiful world. When God made the world, God saw that it was good.

Teach the children the Bible verse, "And God saw that it was good" (Genesis 1:25), in American Sign Language.

Supplies:
none

Zillies®:
none

God — Point the index finger of your right hand, with the other fingers curled down. Bring the hand down and open the palm.

saw — Hold your fingers in a V-shape in front of your eyes. Move the hand forward.

good — Touch the fingers of your right hand to the lips. Move the hand forward and drop it into the open palm of the left hand.

PRESCHOOL 7

Bible Zone Story

Animals

by Sharilyn S. Adair

Have the children sit down in your story area. Tell the children the story and encourage the children to guess the names of the different animals you describe.

In the beginning of everything God made a beautiful world. God made day and night, and they were good. God made the sky and filled it with shiny things like the sun, moon, and stars, and they were good. God made water and land, and they were good. God covered the land with green plants and trees and grasses, and they were good. God filled the water with fishes and sea animals, and God filled the sky with birds. Everything that God made was good. But God was not through.

The land did not yet have creatures on it. God wanted the land to have furry things and sleek, slithery things and bumpy, hairy things. So God made creatures to fill the land.

One creature that God made was small and gray and furry. It had four tiny feet and whiskers and a long, skinny tail. It scurried through the grass and nibbled on seeds.

Can you guess what God made? *(a mouse)* What sound does a mouse make? *(Squeak! Squeak!)*

God made a bigger creature that was furry. It had four feet, floppy ears, a wet nose, and a tail that wagged when the creature was happy. This creature loved to run and to play and to fetch sticks.

What did God make that time? *(a dog)* What sound does a dog make? *(Woof! Woof!)*

God made something even bigger. It was hairy, and it had to bend down to eat grass. It gave milk for other animals to drink.

This time God made what? *(a cow)* What sound do cows make? *(Moo! Moo!)*

Then God made something entirely different. God's new creature didn't have feet and legs. It moved about by slithering on its belly through the grasses and over the rocks. Sometimes when this creature was perfectly still, it looked like a stick on the ground. God made it in several different colors.

Now what did God make? *(a snake)* What sound do snakes make? *(Ssss! Ssss!)*

God made many more wonderful animals. See if you can guess some other animals God made when I make their sound.

Oink! Oink! *(a pig)*
Baaa! Baaa! *(a sheep)*
Ribbit! Ribbit! *(a frog)*
Hee haw! Hee haw! *(a donkey)*

God looked at all the animals, and God saw that they were good.

Who would like to make another animal sound for the class to guess the animal? *(Let the children take turns making animal sounds for the class to guess.)*

In With BZ Bee

Bible Verse Buzz

Choose a child to hold the Bible open to Genesis 1:25.

Say: God made all the animals. The Bible tells us that when God made the animals, God saw that it was good.

Say the Bible verse, "And God saw that it was good" (Genesis 1:25), for the children. Have the children say the Bible verse after you.

Turn your back to the children or hide your hands underneath a table or behind the **BibleZone® FUNspirational® Kit** lid as you place the **BZ Bee puppet** (see page 174) on your hand. Turn around or bring the puppet out where the children can see it.

Pretend to make the puppet talk. Change your voice for the puppet:

Bzzz. Bzzz. Bzzz. Hi, everybody! I'm BZ Bee. *Bzzz. Bzzz. Bzzz.* I like to taste fingers. Do you have fingers? Yum, yum, yum. Let me taste.

Go to each child. Encourage, but do not force, each child to hold up his or her fingers. Have BZ pretend to taste each child's fingers. Have BZ say things like:

Mmmm. Mmmm. You taste like honey. *Bzzz. Bzzz.* You taste like strawberries. *Yumm. Yumm.* You taste like blueberries.

After BZ has tasted each child's fingers, say:

Bzzz. Bzzz. Bzzz. I like to taste your fingers. They're yummy. *(Rub BZ's stomach.)*

Bzzz. Bzzz. Bzzz. I like something else even more than fingers.

I like the Bible. *Bzzz. Bzzz. Bzzz.* Who made all the animals? *(God)* Name some animals God made.

Bzzz. Bzzz. Bzzz. The Bible tells us God made all the animals. When God saw the animals, God saw that it was good.

 **We thank God for all the animals.**

Bzzz. Bzzz. Bzzz. Let's say the Bible verse together.

"And God saw that it was good" (Genesis 1:25).

Have the children repeat the Bible verse with BZ Bee. Have BZ Bee say good-bye to the children. Put the puppet away.

Choose one or more activities to immerse your children in the Bible story.

Supplies:
cassette player

Zillies®:
Cassette

Sing!

lay the song "Made To Praise The Lord" from the **Cassette.** Let the children pretend to be the animals named as the music plays.

Made To Praise The Lord

Ev'ry little bitty critter in the big wide world,
The big wide world, the big wide world,
Ev'ry little bitty critter in the big wide world
Was made to praise the Lord.

Ev'ry squirmy little wormy in the messy mud,
The messy mud, the messy mud,
Ev'ry squirmy little wormy in the messy mud,
Was made to praise the Lord.

Ev'ry bee that ever buzzed,
Ev'ry creature covered with fuzz,
Ev'ry furry feathery, slick or leathery
Animal that ever was
Was made to praise in some most amazing ways.

Ev'ry swishy little fishy in the deep blue sea,
The deep blue sea, the deep blue sea,
Ev'ry swishy little fishy in the deep blue sea,
Was made to praise the Lord.

Ev'ry bee that ever buzzed,
Ev'ry creature covered with fuzz,
Ev'ry furry feathery, slick or leathery
Animal that ever was
Was made to praise in some most amazing ways.

Ev'ry little bitty critter,
Ev'ry squirmy little wormy,
Ev'ry swishy little fishy in the big wide world,
The big wide world, the big wide world,
Ev'ry little bitty critter,
Ev'ry squirmy little wormy,
Ev'ry swishy little fishy in the big wide world,
Was made to praise the Lord.
They were made to praise the Lord.

Writers: Janet McMahan-Wilson and Ted Wilson
© 1992 New Spring Publishing/ASCAP, Bridge Building Music/BMI
All Rights Reserved.
Used by permission of Brentwood-Benson Music Publishing, Inc.

From Brentwood Music Publishing, Inc. recording *God's Way A Song A Day, vol. 2.*

Life Zone

Choose one or more activities to bring the Bible to life.

Turtle Races

Photocopy two copies of the turtle backs **(Reproducible 9B)** and the turtle head, feet, and tail **(Reproducible 9A, bottom)** for each child. Cut out the turtle head, feet, and tail; then set them aside to use later.

Give each child two copies of the turtle backs. Let the children decorate the turtle backs with crayons. Stack the two turtle backs on top of one another. Help each child tape or staple three of the edges together.

Provide recycled newspapers. Show the children how to crumple the newspapers and stuff their turtle backs. Help each child tape or staple the fourth edge of the turtle backs together.

Have the children move to one side of the room and form two lines. Have the first child in each line lie on his or her stomach on the floor. Place the stuffed turtle back on each child's back. Have the children pretend to be turtles and move across the floor to the opposite side of the room, keeping their turtle shells on their backs. Allow some space and then start the next "turtles" on their race. Continue until every child has had a turn.

Say: God created all the animals. God created animals that can run fast, like dogs and tigers. God created animals that move slowly, like turtles. We thank God for all the animals.

Have the children bring their turtle backs to the work table. Give each child a turtle head, feet, and tail. Show the children how to glue or tape the heads, feet, and tails onto the bottoms of their turtle backs.

Supplies:
Reproducibles 9B and 9A (bottom); scissors; crayons; newspapers; glue, tape, or stapler and staples

Zillies®:
none

Four-Fingered Fun

Show the children the **zoo finger puppets** and say the fingerplay.

God made the lions with their mighty roar.
(Hold up the lion finger puppet.)
God made the zebras with their stripes galore.
(Hold up the zebra finger puppet.)
God made the giraffes with their necks so tall.
(Hold up the giraffe finger puppet.)
God made the monkeys that are big and small.
(Hold up the monkey finger puppet.)
Roar, roar, roar, chee, chee, chee!
(Wiggle the lion and monkey finger puppets.)
God made the animals that we see!
(Wiggle all the finger puppets.)

Supplies:
none

Zillies®:
zoo finger puppets

Choose one or more activities to bring the Bible to life.

Supplies:
none

Zillies®:
inflatable celestial ball

Nighttime Prayers

ave the children sit in a circle on the floor. Show the children the **inflatable celestial ball.**

Say: God made our beautiful world. God made the day, and God made the night. God made the sun to shine in the sky during the day. What do we see in the sky at night? *(moon and stars)* **God made the moon and stars that shine at night.** *(Turn off room lights, if possible; whisper.)* **Let's pretend it is nighttime. Let's look up into the sky at the moon and stars.**

Hold the ball up over your head. Sing the song printed below to the tune of "Do You Know the Muffin Man?" Let the children, holding the ball up high, pass the ball around the circle as you sing the song together.

> Do you know God made the moon,
> Made the moon, made the moon?
> Do you know God made the moon,
> And saw that it was good?
>
> Yes, we know God made the moon,
> Made the moon, made the moon.
> Yes, we know God made the moon,
> And saw that it was good.
>
> Do you know God made the stars,
> Made the stars, made the stars?
> Do you know God made the stars,
> And saw that it was good?
>
> Yes, we know God made the stars,
> Made the stars, made the stars.
> Yes, we know God made the stars,
> And saw that it was good.

Pray: Thank you, God, for the moon and stars that shine at night. Thank you, God, for our beautiful world. And thank you, God, for *(name each child).* **Amen.**

Photocopy the **HomeZone®** newsletter to send home to parents.

Home Zone For Parents

Bible Verse
And God saw that it was good.   Genesis 1:25

Bible Story
Genesis 1:24–25

Animals

God created animals to share the earth. There were animals to provide food, clothing, building materials, and transportation. There were animals that played their part in the balance of all of nature. And there were animals that would provide comfort and companionship for human beings.

Help your child understand that she or he shares God's world with animals, and help your child see the importance of being kind to all creatures. Animals have needs of their own, in addition to contributing to our lives. When a child learns to appreciate an animal, he or she learns to treat this animal with respect, and this may carry over to the child's treatment of other people.

Animal-Go-Rounds

apple
peanut butter
animal crackers
pretzel sticks

Cut the apple in half. Each animal-go-round uses half of an apple. Spread peanut butter over the top of the apple. Stand the animal crackers and pretzel sticks in the peanut butter around the apple to represent merry-go-round animals and poles.

Enjoy eating this animal cracker snack with your child. Thank God for apples, peanut butter, crackers—and of course, animals.

We thank God for all the animals.

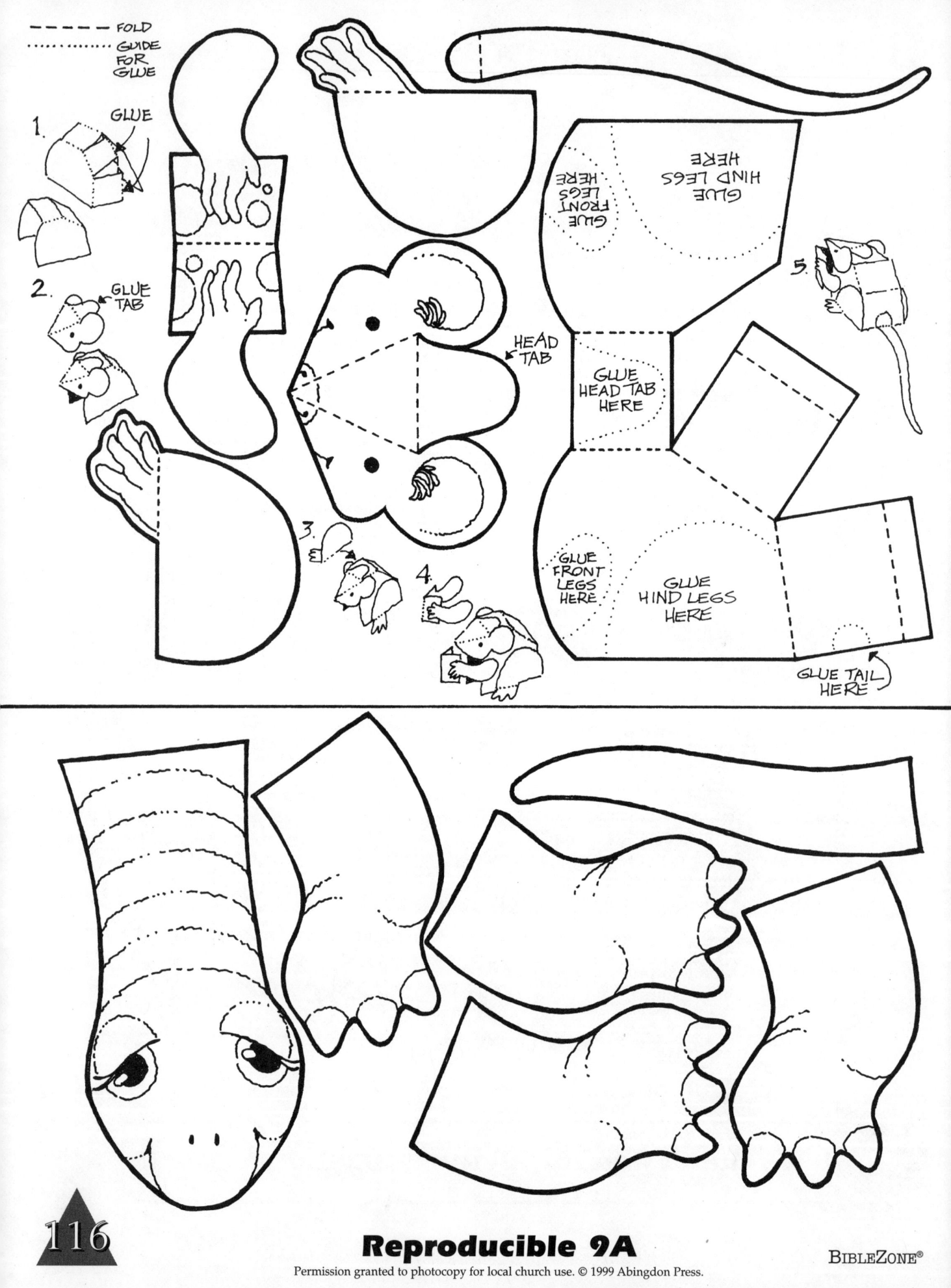

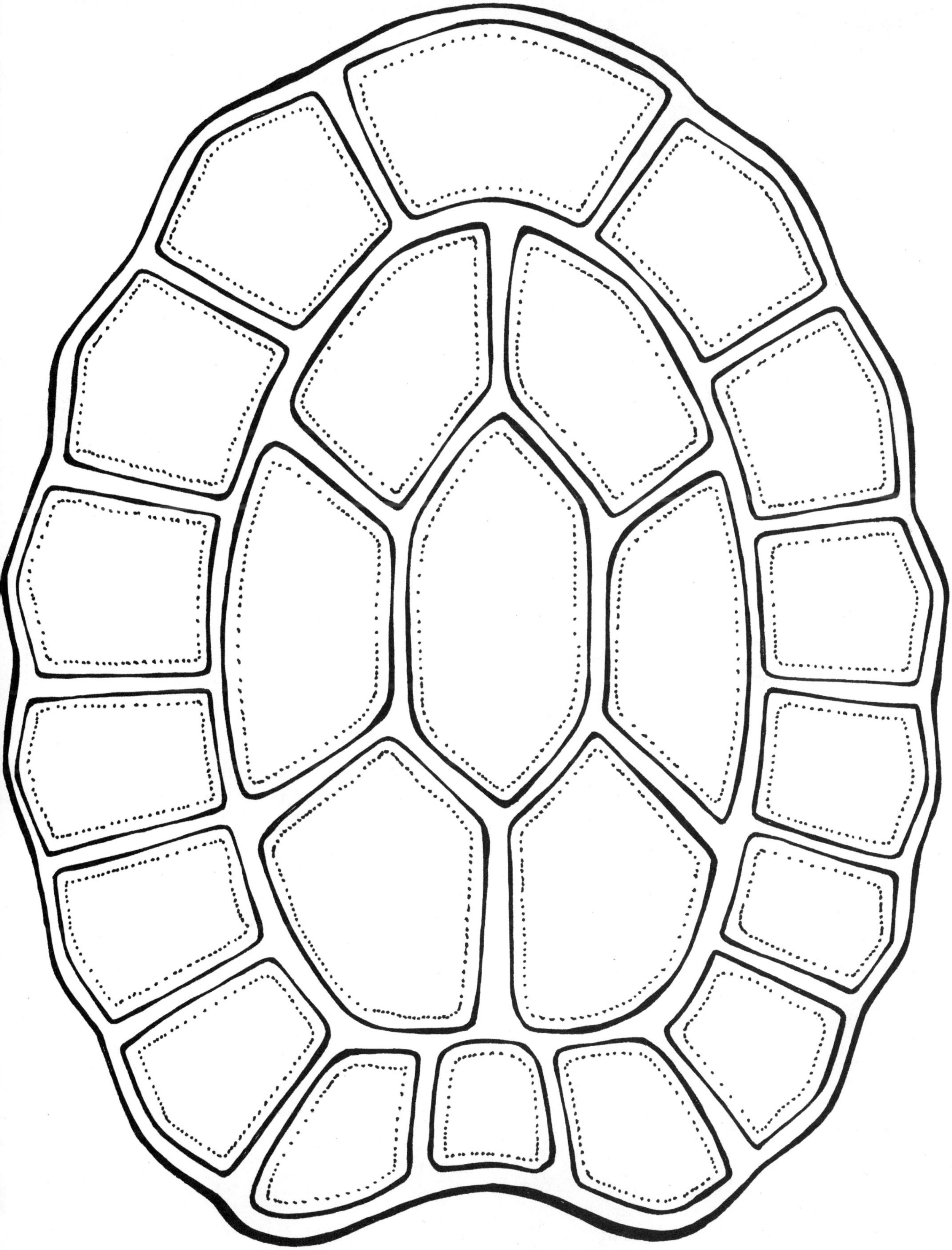

PRESCHOOL 7 **Reproducible 9B**
Permission granted to photocopy for local church use. © 1999 Abingdon Press.

117

10 Bible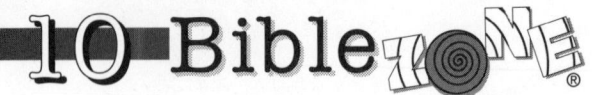

In God's Image

Enter the

Bible Verse
And God saw that it was good.
Genesis 1:25

Bible Story
Genesis 1:26–27

The Creation story in Genesis is so much more than a step-by-step record of the appearance of life on earth. This Scripture is a celebration of human beings—made in the image of God—as the magnificent completion of God's plan of creation.

Humans are different from any of the other living creatures. They share the spiritual characteristics of God that no other creature shares. Humans can think, remember, make plans for the future, choose, create, and reflect on their experiences. Human beings rise above their animal instincts for survival to care about the survival of others. Humans are spiritual beings. They can worship God and can experience feelings of awe and wonder. They can appreciate God's world and can live in fellowship with God, who is Spirit, and with other human beings. Like no other creatures, humans can pray to God and receive and understand God's answers.

When we talk about the image of God, first we have to get beyond the idea of physical characteristics. Obviously, as the children look around themselves, they see people who are a variety of sizes, shapes, and colors.

So, which group, the children will ask, represents the image of God? We will answer, "They all do!" God has given people the ability to choose, not merely to act on instinct or training. The choices humans make determine how they reflect God's image.

Young children are forming self-images that will be with them all their lives. It is important to help young children develop positive self-images. As a teacher you have many opportunities to affirm children. Listen to them. Give them your full attention. Get down on their level and look in their faces. Accept their thoughts and feelings.

Affirm children by constantly reminding them that they are loved. Model God's love through your actions and words. Constantly "catch" children doing things right.

We thank God for people.

Scope the Zone

ZONE	TIME	SUPPLIES	ZILLIES®
Zoom Into the Zone			
Fishy Fun	10 minutes	none	inflatable dolphin ring toss
Thumbody Special	10 minutes	Reproducible 10A, shallow trays, paper towels, tempera paint, smocks, handwashing supplies	
BibleZone®			
Walk This Way	5 minutes	none	none
Sign 'n Say	5 minutes	none	none
In God's Image	10 minutes	none	none
Bible Verse Buzz	5 minutes	Bible, BZ Bee	none
Sing!	5 minutes	cassette player	Cassette
LifeZone			
Picture This	5 minutes	Reproducible 10B, scissors	none
Stand up, Sit Down	5 minutes	none	none
Nighttime Prayers	10 minutes	none	inflatable celestial ball

Zillies® are found in the **BibleZone® FUNspirational® Kit.**

Zoom Into the Zone

Choose one or more activities to catch your children's interest.

Supplies:
none

Zillies®:
Inflatable dolphin ring toss

Fishy Fun

Inflate the **dolphin** and place it in an open area of the room. Have the children line up in front of the dolphin. Let the line begin fairly close to the dolphin.

Give the first child one of the rings. Let the child try to toss the ring over the dolphin's nose. After the toss (whether the child rings the nose or not) have all the children clap their hands and shout, "And God saw that it was good" (Genesis 1:25). Continue until every child has had a turn.

Say: God made fish to swim in the water and birds to fly in the air. But God was not finished. God made many, many more animals. God made animals that crawled and hopped and slithered. God made animals with fur and animals with scales. God made all the animals. But God was not finished. God made something else. Can you guess what else God made? (Let the children respond.) **God made all people!**

We thank God for people.

Supplies:
Reproducible 10A, shallow trays, paper towels, tempera paint, smocks, hand-washing supplies

Zillies®:
none

Thumbody Special

Photocopy the "Look at Me" page **(Reproducible 10A)** for each child.

Say: God made people. (Hold up a hand and wiggle your fingers.) **Each one of us has different fingerprints. Each person is special.**

Have the children wear smocks. Place paper towels in shallow trays. Pour tempera paint on the paper towels to make paint pads. Give each child a "Look at Me" page. Show the children how to press their thumbs and fingers onto the paint pads and then onto their papers to make thumbprints and fingerprints. Let the children make as many prints as they wish on their pages.

Read the poem at the top of the page to the children. Print each child's name in the space provided.

Say: God made (child's name). (Child's name) is special.

Have the children wash their hands. Set the fingerprints aside to dry.

Choose one or more activities to immerse your children in the Bible story.

Walk This Way

Supplies: none

Zillies®: none

Call the children by name either one at a time or in groups of two or three. Instruct the children to move to your story area with one of the following suggestions and sit down.

Pretend you are a baby crawling on the floor.
Pretend you are a girl (or boy) riding a bicycle.
Pretend you are a boy (or girl) jumping rope.
Pretend you are a girl (or boy) swimming in a swimming pool.

Sign 'n Say

Supplies: none

Zillies®: none

Say: **The Bible tells us God made our beautiful world. When God made the world, God saw that it was good.**

Teach the children the Bible verse, "And God saw that it was good" (Genesis 1:25), in American Sign Language.

God — Point the index finger of your right hand, with the other fingers curled down. Bring the hand down and open the palm.

saw — Hold your fingers in a V-shape in front of your eyes. Move the hand forward.

good — Touch the fingers of your right hand to your lips. Move the hand forward and drop it into the open palm of the left hand.

Bible Story

In God's Image

by Sharilyn S. Adair

ave the children sit down in your story area.

Say: In today's story I want you to help celebrate all the good things made by God. Whenever I talk about things being good, I will stop talking for a while. I want you to clap your hands until I raise my hand and start talking again.

In the beginning of everything God made a beautiful world. God worked and worked to make the world just right.

God made the sky and filled it with shiny things like the sun, moon, and stars. And all those things were good. *(Encourage the children to clap their hands.)*

But still God was not through. God made water into oceans and caused land to be separated from the water. And those things were good. *(Encourage the children to clap their hands.)*

But still God was not through. God covered the land with green plants and trees and grasses. And all of those things were good. *(Encourage the children to clap their hands.)*

But still God was not through. God filled the water with fishes and sea animals, and God filled the sky with birds. And those things were good. *(Encourage the children to clap their hands.)*

But still God was not through. God filled the land with all kinds of animals and creepy crawly things. And all those things were good. *(Encourage the children to clap their hands.)*

But still God was not through. "I have created a beautiful world," said God. "But something is missing. I need somebody to take care of my world, somebody who can plant seeds for more plants to grow and who can watch over my trees. I need somebody who can take care of the birds and the fish and the animals. I need somebody *(pause dramatically)* just . . . like . . . me!"

So God made people. God made men and women to take care of the plants and animals and land. And then God was through making the world. And God saw everything that was made, especially the people who were made to be like God. And indeed, everything God had made was very, very good. *(Encourage the children to clap their hands for a longer time.)*

Zone In With BZ Bee

Bible Verse Buzz

hoose a child to hold the Bible open to Genesis 1:25.

Say: God made all people. Each person is special. The Bible tells us that when God made people, God saw that it was good.

Say the Bible verse, "And God saw that it was good" (Genesis 1:25), for the children. Have the children say the Bible verse after you.

Turn your back to the children or hide your hands underneath a table or behind the **BibleZone® FUNspirational® Kit** lid as you place the **BZ Bee puppet** (see page 174) on your hand. Turn around or bring the puppet out where the children can see it.

Pretend to make the puppet talk. Change your voice for the puppet:

Bzzz. Bzzz. Bzzz. Hi, everybody! I'm BZ Bee. *Bzzz. Bzzz. Bzzz.* I like to taste fingers. Do you have fingers? Yum, yum, yum. Let me taste.

Go to each child. Encourage, but do not force, each child to hold up his or her fingers. Have BZ pretend to taste each child's fingers. Have BZ say things like:

Mmmm. Mmmm. You taste like honey.
Bzzz. Bzzz. You taste like strawberries.
Yumm. Yumm. You taste like blueberries.

After BZ has tasted each child's fingers, say:

Bzzz. Bzzz. Bzzz. I like to taste your fingers. They're yummy. (Rub BZ's stomach.)

Bzzz. Bzzz. Bzzz. I like something else even more than fingers.

I like the Bible. *Bzzz. Bzzz. Bzzz.* Who made all the people? (*God*)

Bzzz. Bzzz. Bzzz. The Bible tells us God made all the people. When God saw the people, God saw that it was good.

 **We thank God for people.**

Bzzz. Bzzz. Bzzz. Let's say the Bible verse together.

"And God saw that it was good" (Genesis 1:25).

Have the children repeat the Bible verse with BZ Bee. Have BZ Bee say good-bye to the children. Put the puppet away.

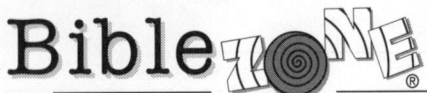

Choose one or more activities to immerse your children in the Bible story.

Supplies:
cassette player

Zillies®:
Cassette

Sing!

 lay the song "If I Were a Butterfly" from the **Cassette.** Let the children pretend to be the animals named.

If I Were a Butterfly

If I were a butterfly
I'd thank You, Lord that I could fly;
And if I were a robin in a tree
I'd thank You, Lord, that I could sing.
And if I were a fish in the sea
I'd wiggle my tail and I'd giggle with glee.
But I just thank you Father for making me me.

'Cause You gave me a heart
And you gave me a smile,
You gave me Lord Jesus
And you made me Your child.
And I just thank you Father for making me me.

If I were an elephant
I'd thank You, Lord by raising my trunk,
And if I were a kangaroo
Oh I'd just hop right up to You.
And if I were an octopus
I'd thank You, Lord for my good looks.
But I just thank you Father for making me me.

'Cause You gave me a heart
And you gave me a smile,
You gave me Lord Jesus
And you made me Your child.
And I just thank you Father for making me me.

If I were a wiggley worm
I'd thank You, Lord that I could squirm;
And if I were a crocodile
I'd thank You, Lord that I could smile.
And if I were a fuzzy, wuzzy bear,
I'd thank You, Lord for my fuzzy, wuzzy hair.
But I just thank You, Father for making me me.

'Cause You gave me a heart
And you gave me a smile,
You gave me Lord Jesus
And you made me Your child.
And I just thank you Father for making me me.
And I just thank You, Father for making me me.

© 1995 New Spring Publishing/ASCAP
All Rights Reserved.
Used by permission of Brentwood-Benson Music Publishing, Inc.

From the Brentwood-Benson Music Publishing, Inc. recording *It's a Great Day to Praise the Lord*.

Choose one or more activities to bring the Bible to life.

Picture This

Photocopy and cut apart the body picture cards **(Reproducible 10B).** Say the poem printed below for the children. Hold up a picture card as indicated in the poem and let the children say the word.

Look at me, look at me,
I am special, as you can see.

I have one _____ *(hold up picture of the nose).*
It's on my face.
I have two _____ *(hold up picture of the legs)*
To run a race.

Look at me, look at me,
I am special, as you can see.

I have two _____ *(hold up picture of the ears)*
To hear you talk.
I have two _____ *(hold up picture of the feet)*
To take a walk.

Look at me, look at me,
I am special, as you can see.

I have two _____ *(hold up picture of the eyes)*
To see the sky.
I have two _____ *(hold up picture of the hands)*
To wave good-bye.

Look at me, look at me,
I am special, 'cause God made me!

Supplies:
Reproducible 10B, scissors

Zillies®:
none

Stand Up, Sit Down

Have the children sit down.

Say: God made people with brown hair. If you have brown hair, stand up. *(Have children with brown hair stand up.)* **Sit down. God made people with blonde hair. If you have blonde hair, stand up.** *(Have children with blonde hair stand up.)* **Sit down**.

Continue naming hair color, eye color, and other physical characteristics until every child has stood up. End by **saying: If God made you, stand up! Sit down! Shout, shout, shout!** *(Have children shout "Hooray!")*

Supplies:
none

Zillies®:
none

Choose one or more activities to bring the Bible to life.

Supplies:
none

Zillies®:
inflatable celestial ball

Nighttime Prayers

ave the children sit in a circle on the floor. Show the children the **inflatable celestial ball.**

Say: God made our beautiful world. God made the day, and God made the night. God made the sun to shine in the sky during the day. What do we see in the sky at night? *(moon and stars)* **God made the moon and stars that shine at night.** *(Turn off room lights, if possible; whisper.)* **Let's pretend it is nighttime. Let's look up into the sky at the moon and stars.**

Hold the ball up over your head. Sing the song printed below to the tune of "Do You Know the Muffin Man?" Let the children, holding the ball up high, pass the ball around the circle as you sing the song together.

> Do you know God made the moon,
> Made the moon, made the moon?
> Do you know God made the moon,
> And saw that it was good?
>
> Yes, we know God made the moon,
> Made the moon, made the moon.
> Yes, we know God made the moon,
> And saw that it was good.
>
> Do you know God made the stars,
> Made the stars, made the stars?
> Do you know God made the stars,
> And saw that it was good?
>
> Yes, we know God made the stars,
> Made the stars, made the stars.
> Yes, we know God made the stars,
> And saw that it was good.

Pray: Thank you, God, for the moon and stars that shine at night. Thank you, God, for our beautiful world. And thank you, God, for *(name each child).* **Amen.**

Photocopy the **HomeZone®** newsletter to send home to parents.

Home Zone For Parents

Bible Verse
And God saw that it was good.   Genesis 1:25

Bible Story
Genesis 1:26–27

In God's Image

God created human beings in God's image. Humans are different from any of the other living creatures. They share the spiritual characteristics of God that no other creature shares. Humans can think, remember, make plans for the future, choose, create, and reflect on their experiences. They can care for one another, and they can worship God.

Young children are forming self-images that will be with them all their lives. It is important to help young children develop positive self-images. You have many opportunities to affirm your child. Listen to your child. Give him or her your full attention. Accept your child's thoughts and feelings.

Affirm your child by constantly reminding your child that he or she is loved. Model God's love through your action and words. Constantly "catch" your child doing things right.

Thumbprint Cookies

1 package vanilla wafer cookies
⅔ cup clear Karo syrup
2 tablespoons vanilla
½ cup jelly or preserves

Place vanilla wafer cookies into a large resealable plastic bag. Securely close bag. Let your child crush the wafers into crumbs. Pour crumbs into a large mixing bowl. Combine syrup and vanilla. Pour over crumbs and mix with hands. Shape crumbs into one-inch balls and place them on a baking sheet. Let your child press a thumb into the center of each ball to make an indentation. Spoon jelly or preserves into the indentation. Cover and chill for one hour before serving.

Remind your child that God made people. Each person is different. Each person is special.

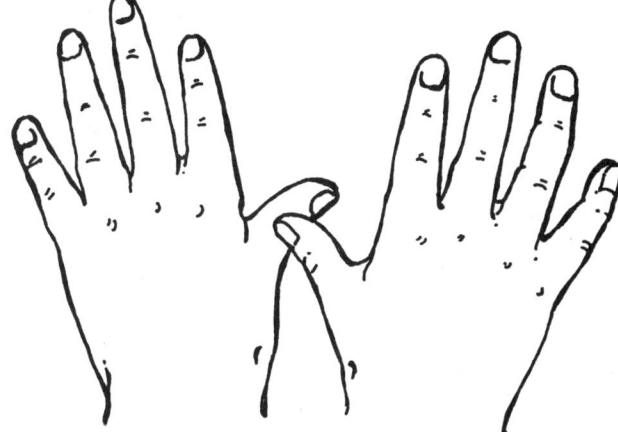

We thank God for people.

Look at me, look at me.
I am special 'cause God made me!

name

Reproducible 10A

Permission granted to photocopy for local church use. © 1999 Abingdon Press.

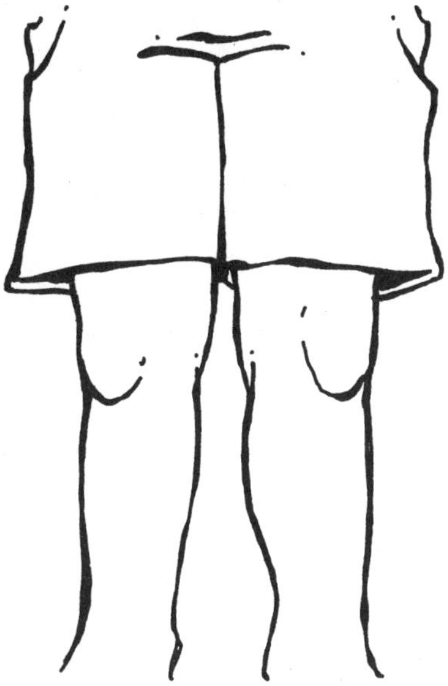

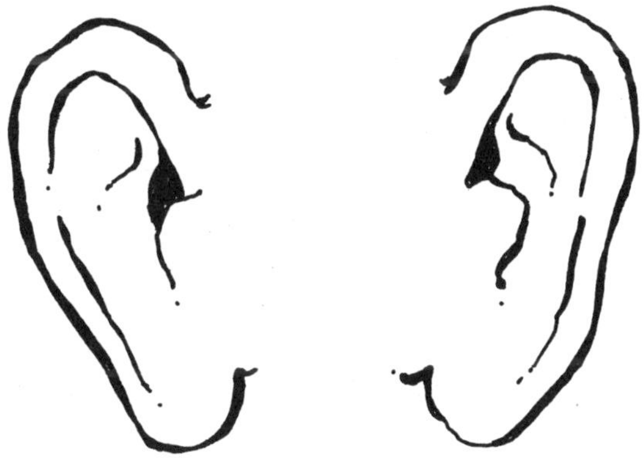

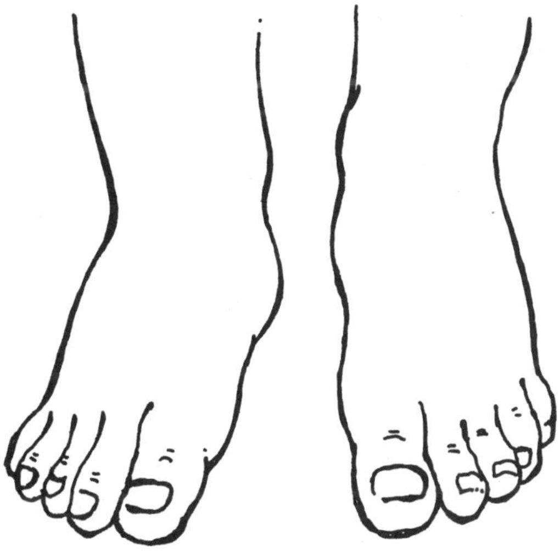

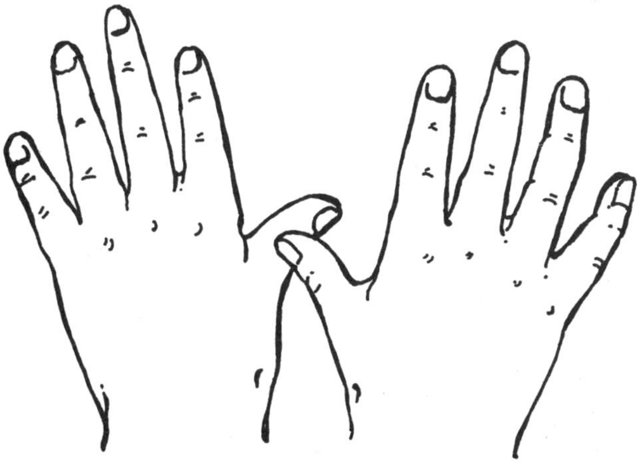

Reproducible 10B

11 Bible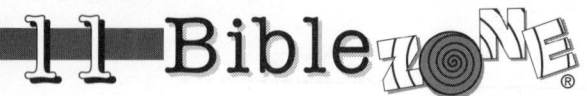

Adam and Eve

Enter the

Bible Verse
God made us, and we belong to God.
Psalm 100:3, *Good News Bible*, adapted

Bible Story
Genesis 2:4–23

In the Book of Genesis a careful reader will discover that there are actually two creation stories. The first story (Genesis 1:1–2:4) culminates with the creation of human beings as one act (Genesis 1:27) and the directive to have dominion over all that God created. In the second creation story (Genesis 2:5–4:26), the creation of humankind is in two stages, but is not complete until man and woman are standing in partnership with each other.

The story that includes Adam and Eve and the Garden of Eden is a colorful story, filled with rich, memorable images—Adam's formation from the dust of the earth, Eve's creation from one of Adam's ribs, a magnificent garden of delights, a Tree of Life, a wily serpent, and an angel with a fiery sword. Through these stories the Hebrew people tried to answer some of their most basic questions: Why do human beings, created in the image of God, refuse to acknowledge the sovereignty of their Creator? How did evil come into such a perfect creation?

The stories concerning ancient history cannot be regarded as exact factual accounts of the sort that today's modern historian or scientist might produce. They *are* historical in that they communicate, however, the *meaning* of history. The writer of these stories emphasized that God was the Supreme Ruler of the universe and that all living creatures were dependent upon God. The writer also explained that throughout the life of all humankind, even at the very beginning of things, human beings have always been a rebellious and prideful lot, quick to turn away from God.

In the second part of the Creation story, the children see a God who is concerned with humanity. This story focuses not on a God who creates with mighty commands, but on one who nurtures from the dust the creature, man, with whom God chooses to be in relationship. This story emphasizes God's loving and caring nature. Children need to know that they are not the results of random acts of science. Of all the living things that God created, only human beings can plan, choose, remember, pray, worship, imagine, and create. Human beings are definitely very special parts of God's creation.

We thank God for people.

Scope the Zone

ZONE	TIME	SUPPLIES	ZILLIES®
Zoom Into the Zone			
Art Show	10 minutes	Reproducible 11A, crayons or markers, masking tape	none
Garden Party	10 minutes	green icing, sugar cones, red cinnamon candies, paper plates, napkins	none
BibleZone®			
Games in the Garden	5 minutes	none	none
Adam 'n Eve March	5 minutes	none	none
Adam and Eve	10 minutes	Reproducible 11A	modeling clay
Bible Verse Buzz	5 minutes	Bible, BZ Bee	none
Sing!	5 minutes	cassette player	Cassette
LifeZone			
Where Is Adam?	15 minutes	Reproducible 11B, scissors; crayons or markers; tape, glue, or stapler, staples	none
Affirmations	5 minutes	none	none
Look 'n See Prayers	10 minutes	none	binoculars

Zillies® are found in the **BibleZone® FUNspirational® Kit**.

Zoom Into the Zone

Choose one or more activities to catch your children's interest.

Supplies:
Reproducible 11A, crayons or markers, masking tape

Zillies®:
none

Art Show

Photocopy the garden picture **(Reproducible 11A)** for each child.

Say: Today our Bible story is about two people named Adam and Eve. God made Adam and Eve.

We thank God for people.

Adam and Eve lived in a beautiful garden. It was a garden where God had planted all kinds of plants and trees, and there were pretty rivers flowing on every side of the garden. The garden was named Eden. Let's make our garden pictures beautiful.

Encourage the children to decorate their garden pictures with crayons or markers. Help each child display his or her picture around the room. Use masking tape to tape the pictures to chairs, tables, and book shelves.

Supplies:
green icing, sugar cones, red cinnamon candies, paper plates, napkins

Zillies®:
none

Garden Party

Purchase green icing (squeeze tubes of icing are less messy), red cinnamon candies, and sugar ice cream cones. Give each child a paper plate and a napkin.

Say: Today our Bible story is about two people named Adam and Eve. Adam and Eve lived in a beautiful garden named Eden. It was a garden where God had planted all kinds of plants and trees. Let's pretend our paper plate is the Garden of Eden. Let's put a tree in our garden.

Squirt a glob of green icing in the center of the paper plate. Press a sugar cone upside down in the glob of icing. Let the children take turns squirting green icing all over their sugar cones. Give each child a few red cinnamon candies. Let the children press the candies into the icing on their trees for fruit.

Say: God made the Garden of Eden, and God made Adam and Eve. God made all people. We thank God for people.

NOTE: Be aware of children with food allergies. Substitute foods as necessary.

Choose one or more activities to immerse your children in the Bible story.

Games in the Garden

Have the children stand in a circle in an open area of the room. Have the children hold hands and walk around the circle as you say the poem printed below. On the last line of each verse, have the children fall down.

Supplies:
none

Zillies®:
none

So God made the first man,
(Walk around the circle.)
The first man, the first man.
So God made the first man,
And Adam was his name.
(All fall down.)

Then God made a garden,
(Walk around the circle.)
A garden, a garden.
Then God made a garden,
And Eden was its name.
(All fall down.)

Then God made a woman,
(Walk around the circle.)
A woman, a woman.
Then God made a woman,
And Eve was her name.
(All fall down.)

Adam 'n Eve March

Lead the children to the story area with the following poem.

Supplies:
none

Zillies®:
none

God made Adam, and God made Eve.
(Turn one hand palm up; turn other hand palm up.)
God made all people in the world, you see.
(Sweep arms in circle.)
So let's march all around the town.
(March with the children to your story area. Repeat this line as necessary.)
Now stretch up tall, then sit right down!
(Stop in story area. Stretch arms overhead; then sit down.)

Bible Zone Story

Adam and Eve

by Sharilyn S. Adair

Have the children bring their garden pictures **(Reproducible 11A)** and sit down around a table. Give each child a lump of **modeling clay** to play with as you tell today's story. Keep a lump for yourself. If you have a large group of children, use the recipe on page 168 to make more clay.

God created a world that was good, and God wanted the good world to be cared for. So God took some clay and made it into the shape of a man who could care for the world. Let's all make our clay into the shape of a man lying down.

After God had shaped the person, God breathed into its nose; and a man named Adam came to life. Let's all make our clay men jump up and run around.

Then God took Adam to a part of the world that was very beautiful. It was a garden where God had planted all kinds of plants and trees, and there were pretty rivers flowing on every side of the garden. The garden was named Eden. God asked Adam to care for the Garden of Eden. *(Place lump of clay on garden picture.)*

Adam liked the Garden of Eden, but he was all alone; and God saw that Adam was lonely. So first God brought Adam some animals to have and to name. Adam named all of the animals, but he was still lonely.

Then God decided that what Adam really needed was a partner. So God made Adam fall asleep. Then God took part of Adam and made that part into a woman named Eve. Let's roll up our clay man and break him into two pieces. Now we can make a man and a woman from the clay.

When Adam woke up and saw Eve, he was happy. Now he would not be alone in the Garden of Eden. Let's make our clay people walk together in the garden. God made Adam and Eve. "God made us, and we belong to God" (Psalm 100:3, *Good News Bible*, adapted).

Zone In With BZ Bee

Bible Verse Buzz

hoose a child to hold the Bible open to Psalm 100:3.

Say: God made Adam and Eve. God made all people. We belong to God.

Say the Bible verse, "God made us, and we belong to God" (Psalm 100:3, *Good News Bible*, adapted), for the children. Have the children say the Bible verse after you.

Turn your back to the children or hide your hands underneath a table or behind the **BibleZone® FUNspirational® Kit** lid as you place the **BZ Bee puppet** (see page 174) on your hand. Turn around or bring the puppet out where the children can see it.

Pretend to make the puppet talk. Change your voice for the puppet:

Bzzz. Bzzz. Bzzz. Hi, everybody! I'm BZ Bee. *Bzzz. Bzzz. Bzzz.* I like to taste fingers. Do you have fingers? Yum, yum, yum. Let me taste.

Go to each child. Encourage, but do not force, each child to hold up his or her fingers. Have BZ pretend to taste each child's fingers. Have BZ say things like:

Mmmm. Mmmm. You taste like honey.
Bzzz. Bzzz. You taste like strawberries.
Yumm. Yumm. You taste like blueberries.

After BZ has tasted each child's fingers, say:

Bzzz. Bzzz. Bzzz. I like to taste your fingers. They're yummy. (*Rub BZ's stomach.*)

Bzzz. Bzzz. Bzzz. I like something else even more than fingers.

I like the Bible. *Bzzz. Bzzz. Bzzz.* Who made Adam and Eve? (*God*) Where did Adam and Eve live? (*Garden of Eden*)

Bzzz. Bzzz. Bzzz. The Bible tells us God made Adam and Eve. God made all people. We belong to God.

 **We thank God for people.**

Bzzz. Bzzz. Bzzz. Let's say the Bible verse together.

"God made us, and we belong to God" (Psalm 100:3, *Good News Bible*, adapted).

Have the children repeat the Bible verse with BZ Bee. Have BZ Bee say good-bye to the children. Put the puppet away.

Choose one or more activities to immerse your children in the Bible story.

Supplies:
cassette player

Zillies®:
Cassette

Sing!

lay the song "If I Were a Butterfly" from the **Cassette.** Let the children pretend to be the animals named.

If I Were a Butterfly

If I were a butterfly
I'd thank You, Lord that I could fly;
And if I were a robin in a tree
I'd thank You, Lord, that I could sing.
And if I were a fish in the sea
I'd wiggle my tail and I'd giggle with glee.
But I just thank you Father for making me me.

'Cause You gave me a heart
And you gave me a smile,
You gave me Lord Jesus
And you made me Your child.
And I just thank you Father for making me me.

If I were an elephant
I'd thank You, Lord by raising my trunk,
And if I were a kangaroo
Oh I'd just hop right up to You.
And if I were an octopus
I'd thank You, Lord for my good looks.
But I just thank you Father for making me me.

'Cause You gave me a heart
And you gave me a smile,
You gave me Lord Jesus
And you made me Your child.
And I just thank you Father for making me me.

If I were a wiggley worm
I'd thank You, Lord that I could squirm;
And if I were a crocodile
I'd thank You, Lord that I could smile.
And if I were a fuzzy, wuzzy bear,
I'd thank You, Lord for my fuzzy, wuzzy hair.
But I just thank You, Father for making me me.

'Cause You gave me a heart
And you gave me a smile,
You gave me Lord Jesus
And you made me Your child.
And I just thank you Father for making me me.
And I just thank You, Father for making me me.

© 1995 New Spring Publishing/ASCAP
All Rights Reserved.
Used by permission of Brentwood-Benson Music Publishing, Inc.

From the Brentwood-Benson Music Publishing, Inc. recording *It's a Great Day to Praise the Lord.*

Choose one or more activities to bring the Bible to life.

Where Is Adam?

Supplies:
Reproducible 11B; scissors; crayons or markers; tape, glue, or staples, stapler

Zillies®:
none

Photocopy and cut apart the Adam and Eve puppets **(Reproducible 11B)** for each child. Give each child both puppets. Let the children decorate the puppets with crayons or markers.

Say: Today our Bible story is about two people named Adam and Eve. God made Adam and Eve.

Show the children how to fold the puppets along the dotted lines. Glue, tape, or staple the sides and tops of the puppets together. Leave the bottom of the puppets open. Show the children how to place their hands inside the puppets.

Have the children hold their puppets behind their backs. Put on a set of puppets and hold the puppets behind your back. Sing the following song to the tune of "Are You Sleeping?" Sing one line and move your puppets. Have the children repeat the line and move their puppets after you.

Where is Adam?	Where is Eve?
Where is Adam?	**Where is Eve?**
Here I am.	Here I am.
(Bring Adam puppet to the front.)	*(Bring Eve puppet to the front.)*
Here I am.	**Here I am.**
(Bring Adam puppet to the front.)	*(Bring Eve puppet to the front.)*
I am in the Garden.	I am Adam's partner.
(Move puppet back and forth.)	*(Move puppet back and forth.)*
I am in the Garden.	**I am Adam's partner.**
(Move puppet back and forth.)	*(Move puppet back and forth.)*
God made me.	God made me.
(Move Adam puppet behind back.)	*(Move Eve puppet behind back.)*
God made me.	**God made me.**
(Move Adam puppet behind back.)	*(Move Eve puppet behind back.)*

Say: God made Adam and Eve. God made all people.

 **We thank God for people.**

PRESCHOOL 7

Choose one or more activities to bring the Bible to life.

Supplies:
none

Zillies®:
none

Affirmations

ave the children sit down on the floor in a circle.

Say: Our Bible verse says, "God made us, and we belong to God" (Psalm 100:3, *Good News Bible,* **adapted). When I point to you and say your name, you say, "We belong to God" back to me.**

Point to a child and **say: God made** *(child's name).*

Have the child **respond: We belong to God.**

Continue around the circle, naming each child and having each child respond.

Supplies:
none

Zillies®:
binoculars

Look 'n See Prayers

ay: **God has made a beautiful world. Let's thank God for the things God has made.**

Show the children the **binoculars** and **say: We use binoculars to look at things. When I give you the binoculars, pretend to look through them and see something God has made.** *(Look though the binoculars).* **I see a rainbow. Thank you, God, for rainbows**.

Give the binoculars to one of the children in the circle. Encourage that child to look through the binoculars and pretend to see something God has made. Have the child name whatever he or she is pretending to see.

Say: Thank you, God, for *(whatever the child names).*

Pass the binoculars around the circle and give each child an opportunity to pretend to see something God has made. After each child's turn thank God for whatever the child named.

Take the binoculars after the last child has had a turn. Look through the binoculars at the children and **say: I see someone God made. I see** *(name all the children).* **Thank you, God, for** *(name all the children.)* **Amen.**

Photocopy the **HomeZone®** newsletter to send home to parents.

Home Zone For Parents

Bible Verse
God made us, and we belong to God.
Psalm 100:3,
Good News Bible, adapted

Bible Story
Genesis 2:4–23

Adam and Eve

Today's Bible story centers around the second account of Creation, the story of Adam and Eve. This story focuses not on a God who creates with mighty commands, but on one who nurtures from the dust the creature, man, with whom God chooses to be in relationship. This story emphasizes God's loving and caring nature.

Children need to know that they are not the results of random acts of science. Of all the living things that God created, only human beings can plan, choose, remember, pray, worship, imagine, and create. Human beings are definitely very special parts of God's creation.

Adam's Apples

apple
peanut butter

Enjoy eating this snack with your child. Core the apple using an apple corer or a knife. Fill the core with peanut butter. Slice the apple horizontally across the core to make thick rings.

Note: An adult will need to core the apple.

Thank God for People

Remind your child that God made all people. Pray with your child, thanking God for the people she or he knows by name.

We thank God for people.

Reproducible 11A

Permission granted to photocopy for local church use. © 1999 Abingdon Press.

Reproducible 11B
Permission granted to photocopy for local church use. © 1999 Abingdon Press.

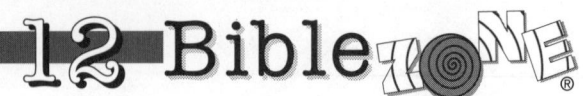

The Naming

Enter the Zone

Bible Verse
O LORD, our LORD,
   your greatness is seen in all the world.
      Psalm 8:1, *Good News Bible*

Bible Story
Genesis 1:28–31; 2:18–20

God did not simply create and then move on. God created, provided, and gave human beings the task of being the caretakers over all that God had created. In the Creation story in the first chapter of Genesis, God gave human beings dominion over creation. In the second chapter of Genesis, God gave Adam the task of caring for the garden and naming all the animals.

When we hear the word *dominion* today, it is easy to think that God has given human beings the power and the authority to control. We often consider *dominion* and *domination* interchangeable. However, the word *dominion* means much more than that. *Dominion* means being responsible for something. In this case human beings are responsible for the care of God's world. We are to act as God's presence in the world. To have dominion means to protect and provide not only for our own needs, but also for the needs of everything that God created. God created human beings to be in partnership with God. As partners, humans have the responsibility of caring for God's earth and God's creatures—including other humans.

Children look at the world with awe and wonder. Everything is a miracle—the birth of a baby bird, the first flowers of spring, the rainbow in the sky. They take the time to appreciate God's wonderful creation. They welcome the responsibility of caring for God's gift. For this reason it is easy to motivate children to participate in environmental activities. Even young children can understand the need to care for plants and animals.

God made people to care for the world.

Scope the Zone

ZONE	TIME	SUPPLIES	ZILLIES®
Zoom Into the Zone			
Animal Mania	10 minutes	Reproducible 12A, scissors	none
Ducks in a Row	10 minutes	dishpan, water; or blue construction paper	plastic ducks
BibleZone®			
Adam, Adam	10 minutes	none	none
Adam 'n Eve March	5 minutes	none	none
Naming	10 minutes	Reproducible 12A, scissors	none
Bible Verse Buzz	5 minutes	Bible, BZ Bee	none
Sing!	5 minutes	cassette player	Cassette
LifeZone			
Mammal Mixup	10 minutes	Reproducible 12B, scissors, construction paper, glue, crayons or markers	none
Who Cares?	5 minutes	none	none
Look 'n See Prayers	10 minutes	none	binoculars

Zillies® are found in the **BibleZone® FUNspirational® Kit.**

Zoom Into the Zone

Choose one or more activities to catch your children's interest.

Supplies:
Reproducible 12A, scissors

Zillies®:
none

Animal Mania

Photocopy and cut apart at least two sets of the animal pictures **(Reproducible 12A)**. Place the cards on the table or rug. Let the children enjoy matching the pictures.

Say: God made our beautiful world. God made people and wanted them to take care of the beautiful world.

God made people to care for the world.

In our Bible story today God told Adam, the first man, to name all the animals. One way we can take care of the world is to take care of animals.

Talk with the children about ways we can take care of animals, such as giving them food and water and handling them carefully.

Supplies:
dishpan, water; or blue construction paper

Zillies®:
plastic ducks

Ducks in a Row

Have the children stand in a line. Place a dishpan partially filled with water or a piece of blue construction paper at the end of the line. Tell the children to pretend that the water or paper is a pond.

Say: God made our beautiful world. God made the plants, and God made the animals. God made people and wanted them to take care of the beautiful world. In our Bible story today God told Adam, the first man, to name all the animals. One way we can take care of the world is to take care of animals.

Show the children one of the **plastic ducks** and **ask: What animal is this?** *(a duck)* **What can we do to take care of ducks?** *(Feed them bread. Make sure the ponds and lakes they swim in are kept clean.)* **What do we need to do to keep the water in the ponds and lakes clean?** *(Don't throw trash into the water.)* **Let's help our ducks find their way to clean water.**

Have the children pass the duck from one child to the next in front of their bodies. Have the last child in the line put the duck in the pond. Have the children pass the next duck in back of their bodies. Continue passing the remaining ducks in a different way (over their heads, between their legs, with their eyes closed, and standing on one leg.)

Bible

Choose one or more activities to immerse your children in the Bible story.

Adam, Adam

Have the children move to lie down on the floor.

Say: God made Adam and Eve and wanted them to take care of the beautiful world God had made. God told Adam to name all the animals. When I say the name of an animal, get up and pretend to be that animal. When I say, "Thank you, God, for animals," lie back down and be still.

Adam, Adam, I see a rabbit.
(Have the children pretend to be rabbits.)
Thank you, God, for animals.
(Have the children lie back down.)

Adam, Adam, I see a bear.
(Have the children pretend to be bears.)
Thank you, God, for animals.
(Have the children lie back down.)

Adam, Adam, I see a duck.
(Have the children pretend to be ducks.)
Thank you, God, for animals.
(Have the children lie back down.)

Adam, Adam, I see a frog.
(Have the children pretend to be frogs.)
Thank you, God, for animals.
(Have the children lie back down.)

Adam, Adam, I see a snake.
(Have the children pretend to be snakes.)
Thank you, God, for animals.
(Have the children lie back down.)

Adam, Adam, I see a cat.
(Have the children pretend to be cats.)
Thank you, God, for animals.
(Have the children lie back down.)

Supplies:
none

Zillies®:
none

Adam 'n Eve March

Lead the children to the story area with the following poem.

God made Adam, and God made Eve.
(Turn one hand palm up; turn other hand palm up.)
God made all people in the world, you see.
(Sweep arms in circle.)
So let's march all around the town.
(March with the children to your story area. Repeat this line as necessary.)
Now stretch up tall, then sit right down!
(Stop in story area. Stretch arms overhead; then sit down.)

Supplies:
none

Zillies®:
none

Naming

by Sharilyn S. Adair

*Photocopy and cut apart the animal pictures **(Reproducible 12A)**. As you introduce each animal in this story, show a picture of it. Let the children giggle and have fun with the silly names that are suggested for the animal. Let them tell you no after each silly name suggestion, but ignore their correct answers at first. After two or three silly suggestions, acknowledge the correct answer they will probably be shouting.*

God made a beautiful world and filled it with animals and birds and fish, and God made people to care for the world. God asked Adam, the first man, to name the animals.

(Show the elephant picture.) Adam saw an animal that looked like this. It was big and gray and had a long trunk for a nose. Look at its big floppy ears. Hmmm. Maybe Adam called this animal a Bigears. Do you think so? *(Pause for a response.)* Or maybe he called it a Lumpty Lump. Have you ever seen a Lumpty Lump? *(Pause for a response.)* Or was it a Snogglenose? *(Pause for a response.)* Oh, of course, it's an elephant. That's a funny name.

(Show the picture of a horse.) Here's another animal Adam named. This animal has four strong legs and long hair called a mane. It can run fast. I guess Adam called it a Runamungus. *(Pause for a response.)* No? Well, maybe it's a Gronk! *(Pause for a response.)* Could it be a Pickle? *(Pause for a response.)* Oh, do you think Adam called it a horse? How silly! A horse!

(Show the snake picture.) Oh, look at this one! I bet Adam called this a Stickywick. *(Pause for a response.)* Or maybe he called it a Snorfle? *(Pause for a response.)* No? Is it a Borgmeister? *(Pause for a response.)* A snake? Adam sure came up with unusual names, didn't he? A snake. My, my.

(Show the picture of a cat.) Oh, look at this one. See the pointed ears? This animal has claws in its feet. If I were Adam, I would call this an Oofda, wouldn't you? *(Pause for a response.)* Would you call it a Snazzle? *(Pause for a response.)* How about a Pittypaws? *(Pause for a response.)* A cat? Think of that!

(Show the pig picture.) Oh, I know what this one must be. Don't you think Adam called it a Flatnose? *(Pause for a response.)* No? Then it must be a Rooter Tooter. *(Pause for a response.)* Is it a Skark? *(Pause for a response.)* It's a pig? Wow! That Adam! He came up with some amazing names.

(Show the giraffe picture.) Here's one more animal. I think Adam called it a Longneck. *(Pause for a response.)* No? How about Spotted Smooze? *(Pause for a response.)* Is it a Hornkle? *(Pause for a response.)* It's a giraffe? Amazing! Adam really knew how to name animals, didn't he?

All animals, whatever their names, are part of God's beautiful world. When God made them, God saw that they were good. God wants us to care for the world and its creatures.

In With BZ Bee

Bible Verse Buzz

hoose a child to hold the Bible open to Psalm 8:1.

Say: God made a beautiful world and filled it with animals and birds and fish, and God made people to care for the world.

Say the Bible verse, "O LORD, our LORD, your greatness is seen in all the world" (Psalm 8:1, *Good News Bible*), for the children. Have the children say the Bible verse after you.

Turn your back to the children or hide your hands underneath a table or behind the **BibleZone® FUNspirational® Kit** lid as you place the **BZ Bee puppet** (see page 174) on your hand. Turn around or bring the puppet out where the children can see it.

Pretend to make the puppet talk. Change your voice for the puppet:

Bzzz. Bzzz. Bzzz. Hi, everybody! I'm BZ Bee. *Bzzz. Bzzz. Bzzz.* I like to taste fingers. Do you have fingers? Yum, yum, yum. Let me taste.

Go to each child. Encourage, but do not force, each child to hold up his or her fingers. Have BZ pretend to taste each child's fingers. Have BZ say things like:

Mmmm. Mmmm. You taste like honey.
Bzzz. Bzzz. You taste like strawberries.
Yumm. Yumm. You taste like blueberries.

After BZ has tasted each child's fingers, say:

Bzzz. Bzzz. Bzzz. I like to taste your fingers. They're yummy. *(Rub BZ's stomach.)*

Bzzz. Bzzz. Bzzz. I like something else even more than fingers.

I like the Bible. *Bzzz. Bzzz. Bzzz.* Who did God ask to name the animals? *(Adam)* Who did God want to take care of the world? *(people)*

Bzzz. Bzzz. Bzzz. The Bible tells us God made a beautiful world and filled it with animals and birds and fish, and God made people to care for the world.

 **God made people to care for the world.**

Bzzz. Bzzz. Bzzz. Let's say the Bible verse together.

"O LORD, our LORD, your greatness is seen in all the world" (Psalm 8:1, *Good News Bible*).

Have the children repeat the Bible verse with BZ Bee. Have BZ Bee say good-bye to the children. Put the puppet away.

Choose one or more activities to immerse your children in the Bible story.

Supplies:
cassette player

Zillies®:
Cassette

Sing!

lay the song "Made To Praise The Lord" from the **Cassette.** Let the children pretend to be the animals named as the music plays.

Made To Praise The Lord

Ev'ry little bitty critter in the big wide world,
The big wide world, the big wide world,
Ev'ry little bitty critter in the big wide world
Was made to praise the Lord.

Ev'ry squirmy little wormy in the messy mud,
The messy mud, the messy mud,
Ev'ry squirmy little wormy in the messy mud,
Was made to praise the Lord.

Ev'ry bee that ever buzzed,
Ev'ry creature covered with fuzz,
Ev'ry furry feathery, slick or leathery
Animal that ever was
Was made to praise in some most amazing ways.

Ev'ry swishy little fishy in the deep blue sea,
The deep blue sea, the deep blue sea,
Ev'ry swishy little fishy in the deep blue sea,
Was made to praise the Lord.

Ev'ry bee that ever buzzed,
Ev'ry creature covered with fuzz,
Ev'ry furry feathery, slick or leathery
Animal that ever was
Was made to praise in some most amazing ways.

Ev'ry little bitty critter,
Ev'ry squirmy little wormy,
Ev'ry swishy little fishy in the big wide world,
The big wide world, the big wide world,
Ev'ry little bitty critter,
Ev'ry squirmy little wormy,
Ev'ry swishy little fishy in the big wide world,
Was made to praise the Lord.
They were made to praise the Lord.

Writers: Janet McMahan-Wilson and Ted Wilson
© 1992 New Spring Publishing/ASCAP, Bridge Building Music/BMI
All Rights Reserved.
Used by permission of Brentwood-Benson Music Publishing, Inc.

From Brentwood Music Publishing, Inc. recording *God's Way A Song A Day, vol. 2.*

Choose one or more activities to bring the Bible to life.

Mammal Mixup

Photocopy and cut apart the animal heads, bodies, and tails **(Reproducible 12B)** for each child. Place the pictures on the work table.

Say: God made our beautiful world. God made the plants, and God made the animals. God made people and wanted them to take care of the beautiful world.

 **God made people to care for the world.**

In our Bible story today God told Adam, the first man, to name all the animals. Let's name some animals. *(Encourage the children to name familiar animals, such as cats, dogs, ducks, and rabbits.)*

Pick one of the animals that the children name and **ask: Does** *(name of animal)* **have fur? feathers? scales? Does it fly in the air? swim in the water? Does it have four legs?**

Show the children the different animal heads, bodies, and tails.

Say: Let's make some pretend animals for us to name.

Give each child a piece of construction paper. Have the children choose an animal body from the pictures you placed on the table. Show the children how to glue the animal body in the middle of their papers.

Then have the children choose animal heads. Have the children glue the animal heads onto the animal bodies.

Finally, have the children choose animal tails. Have the children glue the animal tails onto the animal bodies. Let the children decorate their animals with crayons or markers.

Let each child show her or his animal to the other children. Encourage each child to make up a name for the animal. The names may be nonsense words. Write the animal name on each child's picture.

Supplies:
Reproducible 12B, scissors, construction paper, glue, crayons or markers

Zillies:
none

PRESCHOOL 7

Life Zone

Choose one or more activities to bring the Bible to life.

Supplies:
none

Zillies®:
none

Who Cares?

ay: God made a beautiful world and filled it with animals and birds and fish, and God made people to care for the world.

Say the following rhyme like "Who Stole the Cookies From the Cookie Jar?" Say the first part of the rhyme and name a child. Have that child respond. Repeat the rhyme until everyone has been named.

Teacher: Who can take care of God's beautiful world?
 (Child's name) can take of God's beautiful world.
Child: Who, me?
Everyone: Yes, you!

Supplies:
none

Zillies®:
binoculars

Look 'n See Prayers

ay: God has made a beautiful world. Let's thank God for the things God has made.

Show the children the **binoculars** and **say: We use binoculars to look at things. When I give you the binoculars, pretend to look through them and see something God has made.** (Look though the binoculars.) **I see a rainbow. Thank you, God, for rainbows.**

Give the binoculars to one of the children in the circle. Encourage that child to look through the binoculars and pretend to see something God has made. Have the child name whatever he or she is pretending to see.

Say: Thank you, God, for (whatever the child names.)

Pass the binoculars around the circle and give each child an opportunity to pretend to see something God has made. After each child's turn, thank God for whatever the child named.

Take the binoculars after the last child has had a turn. Look through the binoculars at the children and **say: I see someone God made. I see** (name all the children). **Thank you, God, for** (name all the children). **Amen.**

Photocopy the **HomeZone®** newsletter to send home to parents.

Home Zone For Parents

Bible Verse
O LORD, our LORD, your greatness is seen in all the world.
Psalm 8:1, Good News Bible

Bible Story
Genesis 1:28–31; 2:18–20

The Naming

Today's Bible story centers around the naming of the animals. God did not simply create and then move on. God created, provided, and gave human beings the task of being the caretakers over all that God had created. In the Creation story in the first chapter of Genesis, God gave human beings dominion over creation. In the second chapter of Genesis, God gave Adam the task of caring for the garden and naming all the animals.

Children look at the world with awe and wonder. Everything is a miracle—the birth of a baby bird, the first flowers of spring, the rainbow in the sky. They take the time to appreciate God's wonderful creation. They welcome the responsibility of caring for God's gift. For this reason it is easy to motivate children to participate in environmental activities. Even young children can understand the need to care for plants and animals. Help your child experience caring for God's world by giving your child the responsibility of caring for a plant or animal.

Clay Play

3 cups flour
1 cup salt
1 tablespoon oil
1 cup water with food coloring
mixing bowl

Help your child mix the flour and salt together in the bowl. Gradually add the water and oil. If the mixture is too stiff, add more water. If the mixture is to sticky, add more flour. Store in an airtight container.

Use this recipe to make play dough with your child. Encourage your child to make animals with the dough—and then name them!

God made people to care for the world.

Reproducible 12A
Permission granted to photocopy for local church use. © 1999 Abingdon Press.

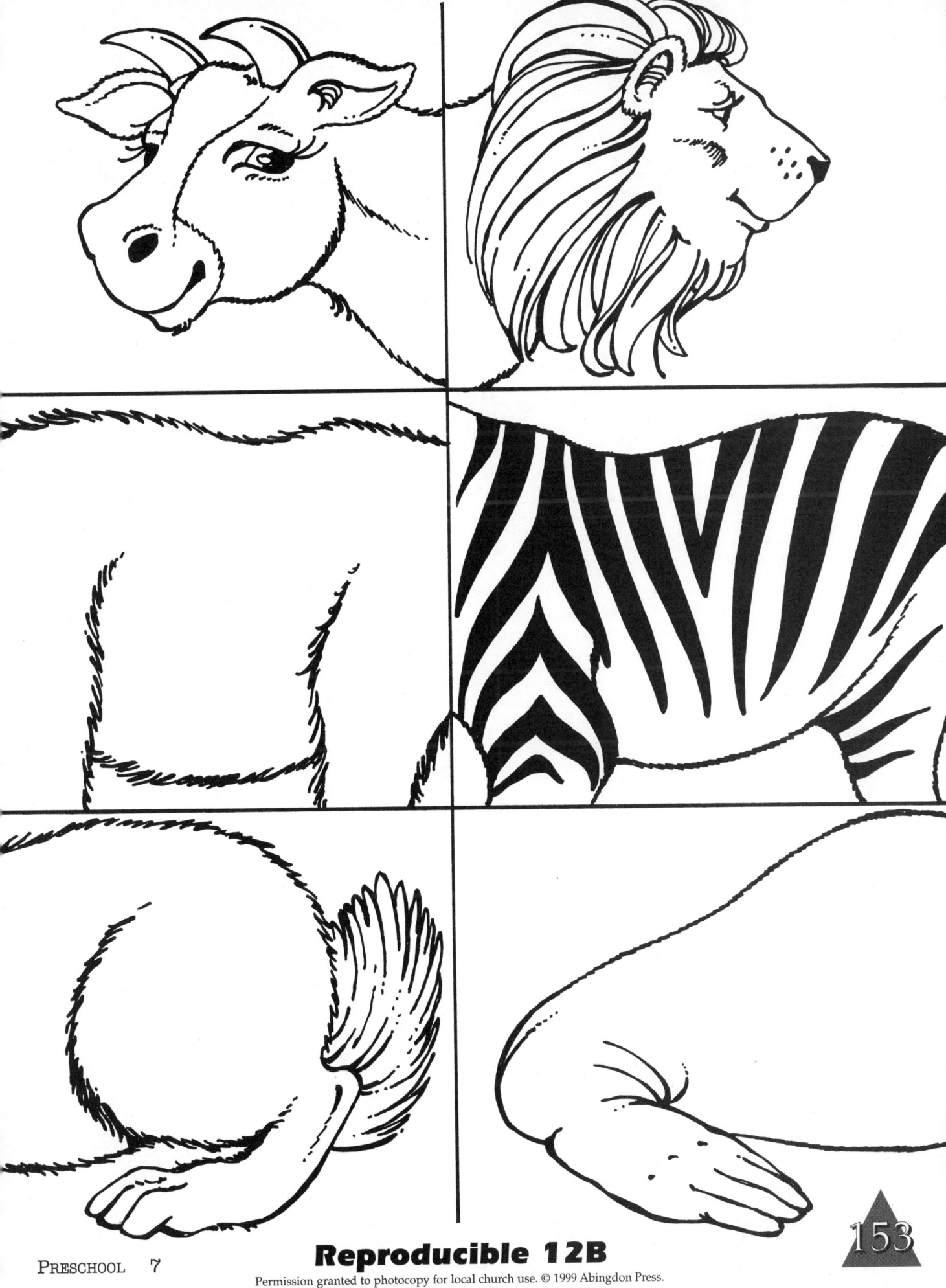

13 Bible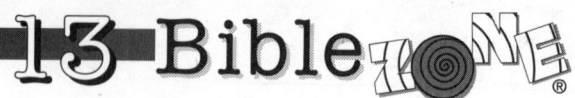

For Everything a Season

Enter the

Bible Verse
For everything there is a season.
Ecclesiastes 3:1

Bible Story
Ecclesiastes 3:1–8

God did not create a temporary, static world. Growth, change, and renewal are a part of God's plan. Seeds are a part of every plant. God told the animals and people to "be fruitful and multiply." God built in the means for a continuing creation. Without this natural process, through which the earth and all that is in it continue to reproduce, life as we know it could not exist.

Song of Solomon, Ecclesiastes, and Psalms celebrate this time of planned renewal—the growing season of spring that comes after the rainy winter, and the rich blessings of each of the seasons. As human beings we are not able to understand the complexity of God's plan for creation, but how reassuring to know that God is definitely in charge!

The cycle of the seasons can be a hard concept for young children to understand. They have not lived long enough to realize that the seasons return year after year. They view time in segments, rather than as an orderly progression of events.

Many children live in areas that do not experience all four seasons. Describe the seasons in terms of your children's experiences. If you live in an area that experiences cold in the winter, talk about hot and cold weather. Ask questions like, "How does snow feel? What do you wear to play in the snow? How do you dress to play in the summer?" If you live in an area that stays warm all year, talk about the seasons as times when certain things happen. In winter, for instance, we celebrate Christmas.

In Genesis 8:22 we have God's promise that the cycle of the days and seasons will continue as long as the earth remains. Remember that in every season of your life, you always can be sure that God loves and cares for you, that the promise of spring is always fulfilled. Pray that the children in your class will learn to trust God through all seasons.

We thank God for the seasons.

Scope the Zone

ZONE	TIME	SUPPLIES	ZILLIES®
Zoom Into the Zone			
Dripdrop Raindrops	15 minutes	Reproducible 13A, crayons or markers; drinking straws, tempera paint, newspapers, smocks; marbles, shallow trays, cup or plastic bowl, spoon, tempera paint, newspapers, smocks; cotton swabs, tempera paint, shallow containers, newspapers, smocks	none
BibleZone®			
Seasons Up	10 minutes	Reproducible 13B, scissors	none
For Everything There Is a Season	10 minutes	none	none
Bible Verse Buzz	5 minutes	Bible, BZ Bee	none
Sing!	5 minutes	cassette player	Cassette
LifeZone			
Four Seasons Frolic	10 minutes	none	none
Winter Games	10 minutes	inexpensive paper plates, cassette player	Cassette
Sing a Song of Seasons	5 minutes	none	none
Look 'n See Prayers	10 minutes	none	binoculars

Zillies® are found in the **BibleZone® FUNspirational® Kit.**

PRESCHOOL 7

Zoom Into the Zone

Choose one or more activities to catch your children's interest.

Supplies:
Reproducible 13A, crayons or markers; drinking straws, tempera paint, newspapers, smocks; marbles, shallow trays, cup or plastic bowl, spoon, tempera paint, newspapers, smocks; cotton swabs, tempera paint, shallow containers, newspapers, smocks

Zillies®:
none

Dripdrop Raindrops

 hotocopy the Bible verse picture (**Reproducible 13A**) for each child. Let the children decorate the pictures with crayons or markers.

Say: The Bible tells us that God made the seasons. Can you name the seasons? *(spring, summer, fall, winter)*

 **We thank God for the seasons.**

Read the Bible verse printed on the picture to the children and have the children repeat it after you.

Ask: What season do you think it is in your picture? *(Pause for response.)* I think the picture shows spring. See the flowers? In the spring God plans for rain to help the flowers grow. Let's add rain to our pictures to help these flowers grow.

Let the children add raindrops to their pictures in one of the following ways:

Dots. Show the children how to use a crayon or marker to make dots on their papers.

Straw painting. Cover the table with newspapers and have the children wear paint smocks. Give each child a straw. Have the children practice blowing through the straw. Place a small glob of blue tempera paint on each child's picture. Show the children how to blow the paint over their pictures.

Marble painting. Cover the table with newspapers and have the children wear paint smocks. Place each child's picture in a shallow tray. Pour blue tempera paint into a cup or plastic bowl. Place a marble into the paint. Use a spoon to take the marble out of the paint and put it on top of the picture in the shallow tray. Show the children how to move the tray to roll the marble over their pictures.

Cotton swab painting. Cover the table with newspapers and have the children wear paint smocks. Pour blue tempera paint into shallow containers. Give the children cotton swabs. Show the children how to dip the cotton swabs into the paint and then touch the swabs onto their pictures to make raindrops. Throw the cotton swabs away when they become saturated with paint.

Set the pictures aside to dry.

Choose one or more activities to immerse your children in the Bible story.

Seasons Up

Photocopy and cut apart the four seasons pictures **(Reproducible 13B)** for each child. Give each child a set of the cards. Have the children sit on the floor or at a table and spread the pictures out in front of them.

Say: God made the seasons. God made fall. In the fall the leaves fall from the trees. Sometimes the wind blows the leaves and the leaves swirl in the air. Find the picture that shows leaves swirling in the air. *(Show the children the picture.)*

God made winter. In the winter the wind turns cold. In some places it snows and snows. Find the picture that shows snow. *(Show the children the picture.)*

God made spring. In spring the rain helps the flowers grow. Find the picture of rain and tiny plants just beginning to grow. *(Show the children the picture.)*

God made summer. In summer it is hot. We can wear shorts when we play in the hot sun. Find the picture of the hot summer sun. *(Show the children the picture.)*

 **We thank God for the seasons.**

Have the children spread their pictures out in front of them again. Say the name of one of the seasons. Have each child find the picture that goes with that season and hold it up. Then have the children repeat the Bible verse, "For everything there is a season" (Ecclesiastes 3:1). Continue until you have named all four seasons several times.

If you want to make the game more active, have the children sit with their pictures on one side of the room. Stand on the opposite side of the room. As you call out the names of the seasons, have the children pick up the correct picture and run across the room to you. Have the children repeat the Bible verse. Have the children return to where they were sitting to continue the game.

Supplies:
Reproducible 13B, scissors

Zillies®:
none

Bible Zone Story

For Everything There Is a Season

by Sharilyn S. Adair

ave the children stand in a circle in your story area.

Say: Today's Bible story is about God's plan for seasons and about how we can see changes in God's world from one season to the next. As you listen to the story poem, watch me and do as I do.

Encourage the children to do the refrain after each verse.

For everything there is a season,
(Hold arms out from sides; turn around.)
Winter, spring, summer, fall.
(Hold up four fingers, one at a time.)
For everything there is a season.
(Hold arms out from sides; turn around.)
We thank God for them all.
(Fold hands in prayer.)

God plans a time just right to plant
The seed for grass to grow.
(Pretend to plant a seed in the ground.)
God plans that when the grass gets tall,
The time is right to mow.
(Hold both hands in front of you as though pushing a mower and say "Rrrr rrr.")
And then God turns the green grass brown
And covers it with snow.
(Make a whooshing sound.)

For everything there is a season,
(Hold arms out from sides; turn around.)
Winter, spring, summer, fall.
(Hold up four fingers, one at a time.)
For everything there is a season.
(Hold arms out from sides; turn around.)
We thank God for them all.
(Fold hands in prayer.)

God plans for springtime rain and flowers;
(Hold your hands above your head and wiggle your fingers as you lower them to waist level.)
God plans for summer sun;
(Make a circle above your head.)
God plans for fall and tumbling leaves,
(Wave your arms back and forth like leaves blowing in the wind.)
For snow and winter fun.
(Hug arms around body as if cold.)
God plans for spring to come again
When wintertime is done.
(Make a circle above your head.)

For everything there is a season,
(Hold arms out from sides; turn around.)
Winter, spring, summer, fall.
(Hold up four fingers, one at a time.)
For everything there is a season.
(Hold arms out from sides; turn around.)
We thank God for them all.
(Fold hands in prayer.)

In With BZ Bee

Bible Verse Buzz

Choose a child to hold the Bible open to Ecclesiastes 3:1.

Say: The Bible tells us that God planned for seasons in our world. God planned for fall, winter, spring, and summer.

Say the Bible verse, "For everything there is a season" (Ecclesiastes 3:1), for the children. Have the children say the Bible verse after you.

Turn your back to the children or hide your hands underneath a table or behind the **BibleZone® FUNspirational® Kit** lid as you place the **BZ Bee puppet** (see page 174) on your hand. Turn around or bring the puppet out where the children can see it.

Pretend to make the puppet talk. Change your voice for the puppet:

Bzzz. Bzzz. Bzzz. Hi, everybody! I'm BZ Bee. *Bzzz. Bzzz. Bzzz.* I like to taste fingers. Do you have fingers? Yum, yum, yum. Let me taste.

Go to each child. Encourage, but do not force, each child to hold up his or her fingers. Have BZ pretend to taste each child's fingers. Have BZ say things like:

Mmmm. Mmmm. You taste like honey.
Bzzz. Bzzz. You taste like strawberries.
Yumm. Yumm. You taste like blueberries.

After BZ has tasted each child's fingers, say:

Bzzz. Bzzz. Bzzz. I like to taste your fingers. They're yummy. *(Rub BZ's stomach.)*

Bzzz. Bzzz. Bzzz. I like something else even more than fingers.

I like the Bible. *Bzzz. Bzzz. Bzzz.* Who made the seasons? *(God)* What are the names of the four seasons? *(fall, winter, summer, spring)*

Bzzz. Bzzz. Bzzz. The Bible tells us God made the seasons.

We thank God for the seasons.

Bzzz. Bzzz. Bzzz. Let's say the Bible verse together.

"For everything there is a season" (Ecclesiastes 3:1).

Have the children repeat the Bible verse with BZ Bee. Have BZ Bee say good-bye to the children. Put the puppet away.

Bible

Choose one or more activities to immerse your children in the Bible story.

Supplies:
cassette player

Zillies®:
Cassette

Sing!

ay: God made the seasons. God made fall, winter, spring, and summer. In the spring we can feel the rain and watch the flowers grow.

Sing the song "God Made the Flowers" from the **Cassette**. The tune is "Go Tell Aunt Rhoady."

God Made the Flowers

God made the warm earth,
God made the warm earth,
God made the warm earth to help the flowers grow.

God made the flowers,
God made the flowers,
God made the flowers so beautiful to see.

God sends the raindrops,
God sends the raindrops,
God sends the raindrops to help the flowers grow.

God made the flowers,
God made the flowers,
God made the flowers so beautiful to see.

God makes the sunshine,
God makes the sunshine,
God makes the sunshine to help the flowers grow.

God made the flowers,
God made the flowers,
God made the flowers so beautiful to see.

Writer: Pam Andrews
© 1993 New Spring Publishing/ASCAP
All Rights Reserved.
Used by permission of Brentwood-Benson Music Publishing, Inc.

From the Brentwood-Benson Music, Inc. recording *Kid's Musical Yearbook*.

Choose one or more activities to bring the Bible to life.

Four Seasons Frolic

Supplies: none

Zillies®: none

Have the children move to an open area of the room.

Say: The Bible tells us God made the seasons. God made summer. Let's make the summer sun. *(Make a circle above your head.)* **God made fall. Let's make the leaves blowing in the wind.** *(Sweep arms around body.)* **God made spring. Let's make the spring rain.** *(Hold your hands above your head and wiggle your fingers as you lower them to waist level.)* **God made winter. The air turns cold in winter.** *(Hug yourself as if you are cold.)* **Listen as I say the name of one of the seasons. When I say the name, quickly make the motion that goes with the season.**

Say the name of each season and have the children do the corresponding motion. Mix up the order of how you name the seasons. Say the names faster and faster.

Winter Games

Supplies: inexpensive paper plates, cassette player

Zillies®: Cassette

Have the children move to an open area of the room. Play one or more of the following games with the children.

Say: The Bible tells us that God made the seasons. Can you name the seasons? *(spring, summer, fall, winter)* **God made winter. In some places winter is cold and there is snow. Let's pretend it's winter. Brrr. It's cold! It's so cold, water turns to ice.**

Freeze Tag. Choose a child to be "winter." Have the remaining children pretend to be water and move around the room. Winter tries to freeze the water. When winter tags a child, the child must freeze or be very still. Let the children take turns being winter.

Ice Skating. Give each child two inexpensive paper plates. Have the children put the paper plates on the rug and then stand on them. Encourage the children to skate around the room by sliding their feet. Play music from the **Cassette** and let the children pretend to ice skate.

Note: For safety reasons, have the children pretend to skate only on a rug.

Snow angels. Have the children lie down on the floor and pretend to make snow angels.

PRESCHOOL 7

161

Life Zone

Choose one or more activities to bring the Bible to life.

Supplies:
none

Zillies®:
none

Sing a Song of Seasons

 ay: The Bible tells us that God made the seasons. We thank God for the seasons.

Sing the Bible verse with the children to the tune of "Do You Know the Muffin Man?"

**For everything there is a season,
Is a season, is a season.
For everything there is a season,
God made them all.**

Supplies:
none

Zillies®:
binoculars

Look 'n See Prayers

 ay: God has made a beautiful world. Let's thank God for the things God has made.

Show the children the **binoculars** and **say: We use binoculars to look at things. When I give you the binoculars, pretend to look through them and see something God has made.** *(Look though the binoculars.)* **I see a rainbow. Thank you, God, for rainbows**.

Give the binoculars to one of the children in the circle. Encourage that child to look through the binoculars and pretend to see something God has made. Have the child name whatever he or she is pretending to see.

Say: Thank you, God, for *(whatever the child names).*

Pass the binoculars around the circle and give each child an opportunity to pretend to see something God has made. After each child's turn thank God for whatever the child named.

Take the binoculars after the last child has had a turn. Look through the binoculars at the children and **say: I see someone God made. I see** *(name all the children)*. **Thank you, God, for** *(name all the children).* **Amen.**

Photocopy the **HomeZone®** newsletter to send home to parents.

Home Zone For Parents

Bible Verse
For everything there is a season. Ecclesiastes 3:1

Bible Story
Ecclesiastes 3:1–8

For Everything a Season

Today your child learned about God's plan for the seasons. An important message of this week's Scripture is that God is in control of the world. God's plan for an orderly world with a time for everything helps to reassure us of God's continuing love and care.

Many children live in areas that do not experience all four seasons. Describe the seasons in terms of your child's experiences. If you live in an area that experiences cold in the winter, talk about hot and cold weather. Ask questions like, "How does snow feel? What do you wear to play in the snow? How do you dress to play in the summer?" If you live in an area that stays warm all year, talk about the seasons as times when certain things happen. In winter, for instance, we celebrate Christmas.

Remember that in every season of your life, you can always be sure that God loves and cares for you and your child.

Ice Cream in a Bag

Remind your child that in summer the weather is hot and we enjoy cold things to eat and drink. Enjoy this cool summer's treat with your child.

1 cup milk
1 tablespoon sugar
1 teaspoon vanilla
ice
gallon-size resealable plastic bag
quart-size resealable plastic bag
salt

Pour milk, sugar, and vanilla in a quart-size resealable plastic bag. Seal the bag securely. Fill the gallon-size resealable plastic bag with ice. Place 6 tablespoons of salt on top of the ice. Place the quart-size bag inside the gallon-size bag and seal the gallon-size bag securely. Shake the bags for about four to five minutes until the ingredients become thick like ice cream. Remove the ice cream from the quart-size bag and eat quickly.

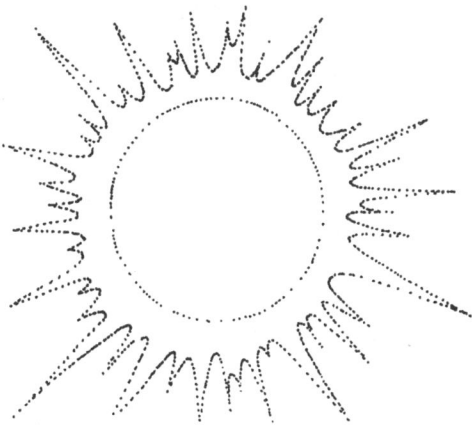

We thank God for the seasons.

PRESCHOOL 7 — Permission granted to photocopy for local church use. © 1999 Abingdon Press.

For everything there is a season.
Ecclesiastes 3:1

Reproducible 13A

Permission granted to photocopy for local church use. © 1999 Abingdon Press.

BibleZone®

Reproducible 13B

Permission granted to photocopy for local church use. © 1999 Abingdon Press.

Birthday Zone

Birthday Cheer

Use the suggestions in this Birthday Zone to celebrate birthdays. Have the children make a circle around the birthday child. Let the children walk in a circle around the child as you say:

> Hip, hip, hooray,
> It's *(child's name)*'s special day.
> Let's gather near
> And give a cheer.
> Hip, hip, hooray!

Have the children stop walking, jump up, and cheer for the child.

Birthday Jingle

Sing this song to the tune of "This Is the Way" to celebrate a child's birthday.

This is the way we light the candles,
Light the candles, light the candles.
This is the way we light the candles
On our birthday cake.

1, 2, 3, 4
(Count the number of candles for the child's age. Hold up a finger for each candle. Pretend to light the tip of each finger.)

Our friend *(child's name)* is four *(use correct age)* today,
Four today, four today.
Our friend *(child's name)* is four today,
Happy birthday, *(child's name)*.

Birthday Buzz

Show the children the **BZ Bee puppet**. Pretend to fly the puppet around the room as you **say**:

> BZ Bee is buzzing
> All around the room.
> He's buzzing to the birthday girl *(boy)*.
> Zoom, zoom, zoom.

Stop at the birthday child and have BZ Bee give the child a hug.

BibleZone®

Clay Zone

Uncooked Clay

3 cups flour
1 cup salt
1 tablespoon oil
1 cup water with food coloring
mixing bowl and spoon

Help your children mix the flour and salt together in the bowl. Gradually add the water and oil. If the mixture is too stiff, add more water. If the mixture is too sticky, add more flour. Store in an airtight container.

Cooked Clay

1 cup flour
1 cup water
½ cup salt
1 tablespoon cream of tartar
few drops of food coloring

Mix dry ingredients together. Mix water and food coloring together. Combine dry and wet ingredients together in a pan and cook on high. Stir constantly. Remove from heat when play dough becomes rubbery with a slightly salty crust. Cool. Knead until smooth. Store in an airtight container.

Song Zone

*et the children listen to the song "The Bible Zone" from the **Cassette** as they enter the room or while working on lesson activities.*

The Bible Zone

Where else can we find a lesson learned on every page?
Stories that have lived to teach us all from age to age.
From the flood to parting waters, burning bushes,
   prophets, scholars,
God's Word takes us anywhere.

In the Bible zone where God's Word comes to life.
In the Bible zone our path is always bright.
A book for all creation to every boy and girl.
In the Bible zone is God's treasure for the world.

In the Bible zone where God's Word comes to life.
In the Bible zone our path is always bright.
A book for all creation to every boy and girl.
In the Bible zone is God's treasure for the world.

Learning of forgiveness or when learning how to pray,
God's Word gives examples of the things we face each day.
When we choose to look inside, we see ahead or back in time.
God's Word takes us anywhere.

In the Bible zone where God's Word comes to life.
In the Bible zone our path is always bright.
A book for all creation to every boy and girl.
In the Bible zone is God's treasure for the world.

In the Bible zone where God's Word comes to life.
In the Bible zone our path is always bright.
A book for all creation to every boy and girl.
In the Bible zone is God's treasure for the world.

Words by David Hampton
© 1997 New Spring Publishing, Inc. (ASCAP)
A div. of Brentwood-Benson Music, Inc. All rights reserved. Used by permission.

Song Zone

Sing for Joy

Use the songs in this **SongZone** when you need a few minutes to get the wiggles out. All the songs are to familiar tunes.

God Made All the World

Sing this song to the tune of "This Old Man."

God made birds, God made bees,
God made monkeys in the trees.
Great big whales and even tiny fleas,
God made all the world, you see.

© 1997 Abingdon Press

The Creation

Sing this song to the tune of "This Is The Way."

God made the sun and moon and stars,
Moon and stars, moon and stars.
God made the sun and moon and stars,
And saw that it was good.

God made the earth and sky and seas,
Sky and seas, sky and seas.
God made the earth and sky and seas.
And saw that it was good.

God made the seeds and plants and trees,
Plants and trees, plants and trees.
God made the seeds and plants and trees,
And saw that it was good.

God made the fish and birds and bees,
Birds and bees, birds and bees.
God made the fish and birds and bees,
And saw that it was good.

God made cows and creeping things,
Creeping things, creeping things.
God made cows and creeping things,
And saw that it was good.

God made people like you and me,
You and me, you and me.
God made people like you and me,
And saw that it was good.

God rested on the seventh day,
Seventh day, seventh day.
God rested on the seventh day,
For it was very good.

© 1997 Abingdon Press

Snack Zone

Tasty Treats

Let the children make and enjoy snacks. Talk about the Bible story as you make and eat the treats. Each recipe is easy for young children to make with a little help from you. And each of these recipes relates to a Bible story in this BibleZone® unit.

Flower Power

strawberries or grapes
apple slices or orange slices
paper plates

Place a strawberry or a few grapes in the center of a plate. These make the center of the flower. Arrange apple slices or orange sections around the strawberry or grapes to make the petals of the flower.

Let the children pretend to be bumblebees buzzing from flower to flower. Let the children fly to enjoy their snacks.

Gingerbread People

½ cup shortening
⅓ cup sugar
½ cup molasses
¼ cup water
2½ cups all-purpose flour
½ teaspoon baking soda
¾ teaspoon ginger
¼ teaspoon cinnamon
raisins
baking sheet
extra flour
rolling pin
people cookie cutters

Prepare dough before class. Cream shortening and sugar. Blend molasses, water, flour, soda, ginger, nutmeg, and cinnamon. Cover and chill 2 to 3 hours.

Heat oven to 350 degrees.

Sprinkle flour on the tabletop. Let the children take turns rolling the dough on the floured surface. The dough should be about ¼-inch thick. If the dough is sticky, add flour. Help the children cut the dough with people cookie cutters. Place the shapes on an ungreased baking sheet. Let the children decorate the cookies with raisins.

Bake 10 minutes. Immediately remove from baking sheet. Turn off oven. Cool. Makes about fifteen 4-inch cookies.

Remind the children that God made people.

PRESCHOOL 7

Permission granted to photocopy for local church use. © 1999 Abingdon Press.

All About

_____
(Child's name)

Parent's Name_____

Address_____

_____Telephone Number_____

Child's Birthday_____Age_____

Child's Brothers and Sisters:

Name_____Age_____

Name_____Age_____

Name_____Age_____

Grandparents or other relatives your child sees often and is close to
_____
_____

Nursery school, daycare, or other programs your child attends
_____
_____

Allergies or situations in your child's life that the teacher should know
_____
_____

Parents will be at
_____

BUZZ Into the Bible Zone®

B U Z Z

Make Learning Bible Verses FUNspirational® with BZ Bee.

Catch your children's interest with this delightful hand puppet.
It's soft!
Its mouth moves!

BZ Bee is two colors children love — hot pink and purple.

BZ Bee is part of every lesson for the first year of BibleZone® (52 lessons).

It's durable!

Buzz to your local Christian bookstore and find me for $29.95. See you in the BibleZone®!

Abingdon Press

BibleZone 7 — Comments From Users

Use the following scale to rate BibleZone® resources.
If you did not use a section, write "Did not use" in the Comments space.

1 = In No Lessons   2 = In Some Lessons   3 = In Most Lessons   4 = In All Lessons

1. *Enter the Zone* provided information that helped me teach this lesson's Scripture.
   1   2   3   4   Comments:

2. The *Scope the Zone* chart made lesson planning easy.
   1   2   3   4   Comments:

3. The teaching plan was organized in a way that made it easy to use.
   1   2   3   4   Comments:

4. The Teacher's Guide provided easy-to-follow instructions for the learning activities.
   1   2   3   4   Comments:

5. The supplies necessary to do the activities were easily located in my home or church.
   1   2   3   4   Comments:

6. My students were able to understand the lesson's ZoneIn®.
   1   2   3   4   Comments:

7. The activities matched the learning level and abilities of my students.
   1   2   3   4   Comments:

8. The number of activities in the lesson plan worked for the time I had available (indicate how much time):_____.
   If not, check:_____ too many _____too few.
   1   2   3   4   Comments:

9. I used activities from the BirthdayZone section of the Teacher's Guide.
   1   2   3   4   Comments:

10. I used activities from the SnackZone section of the Teacher's Guide.
    1   2   3   4   Comments:

11. I used activities from the SongZone section of the Teacher's Guide.
    1   2   3   4   Comments:

12. I used the Cassette in my classroom.
    1   2   3   4   Comments:

13. I used items from the BibleZone® FUNspirational® Kit.
    1   2   3   4   Comments:

14. I sent the HomeZone® page home to parents.
    1   2   3   4   Comments:

15. I used the BZ Bee puppet with my class.
    1   2   3   4   Comments:

ADDITIONAL COMMENTS

Activities my students enjoy the most are:

Activities my students enjoy the least are:

I use BibleZone® for _____ Sunday School _____ Second-Hour Sunday School _____ Children's Church

_____ Wednesday nights _____ Sunday nights _____ Children's Fellowship _____ other

ABOUT MY CLASS

Number of children at each age in my class:

_____ Age 3 _____ Age 4 _____ Age 5

_____ Other (Specify) _____

Average number of children who attend my class each week: _____

I teach: _____ alone _____ with another teacher each week

_____ taking turns with other teachers _____ with an adult helper

ABOUT MY CHURCH

_____ Rural _____ Small Town _____ Downtown _____ Suburban

_____ Under 200 Members _____ 200-700 Members _____ Over 700 Members

Church Name and Address: _____

_____

My Name and Address: _____

_____

Please return this form to: Amy Smith
Research Department
201 8th Ave., So.
P.O. Box 801
Nashville, TN 37202-0801